Y0-CAW-928

Travels in New England

Travels in
NEW ENGLAND

Volumes I & II

BASED ON TIMOTHY DWIGHT'S
TRAVELS IN NEW-ENGLAND AND NEW-YORK

Photographs by Katharine Knowles
Text by Thea Wheelwright

BARRE PUBLISHING · BARRE, MASSACHUSETTS · 1977
DISTRIBUTED BY CROWN PUBLISHERS, INC.

Frontispiece:
Wood road, Salisbury, Connecticut

NOTE TO THE READER:
Volume I first appeared as a separate publication.

Library of Congress Cataloging in Publication Data
Knowles, Katharine Travels in New England.
"First edition, volumes I and II combined;
volume I appeared separately in 1972."
Includes index.
1. New England – Description and travel – 1951– – Views.
2. New England – Description and travel – 1775–1865.
3. Dwight, Timothy, 1752–1817.
I. Wheelwright, Thea. II. Dwight, Timothy, 1752–1817.
Travels in New England and New York. III. Title.
F5.K65 1977 917.4'04'40222 77-21644
ISBN 0-517-52909-2

Published simultaneously in Canada by General Publishing Company Limited
First edition Volumes I and II combined;
Volume I appeared separately in 1972.
Printed in the United States of America

Contents

Introduction

A POTENTIAL photographic composition lies ready to be developed from every vista upon which Katharine Knowles allows her eyes to linger. Book after book illustrated or dominated by her work has found delighted owners who share her love of the visual.

Miss Knowles has illustrated particular aspects of several New England states. Her publishers conceived the idea of the whole region as subject for her next photographic essay—but where to find an authoritative accompaniment, short of enormous research as well as travel?

The answer lay at hand in four volumes of "letters" written to an imaginary British gentleman provided with a rather jaundiced view of the American colonies by his creator, Timothy Dwight, president of Yale University and indefatigable traveler in New England. These were published early in the nineteenth century in obedience to Dwight's dying wish.

The first journey he recorded took place nearly two hundred years ago, but in spite of all the changes that have evolved since then, New England is still herself, land and sea. Thus Dwight's *Travels in New-England and New-York** could, in a sense, illuminate Katharine Knowles's contemporary photographs.

It is safe to say that Timothy Dwight examined with a set purpose in mind a wider area of the United States, in greater detail, over a longer period of years, than any other person in his time.

He was concerned with the discovery and preservation of New England origins. He wanted to give the New Englander of his day not only a feeling for his land, but an appreciation of its development from a state of wilderness toward civilization.

That same concern for origins has reached new depth in our time, when the results of man's technology plus his careless waste are so defacing the land in many areas as to make it unrecognizable to one who had seen it at the beginning. The government and alert individuals are promoting conservation of what is left, at least, even if much is lost beyond redemption.

It is not far-fetched to say that the work of Katharine Knowles is part of the same pursuit, for her photographs catch and hold a beauty still to be found in New England. She has followed Dwight's itineraries where possible, including as much as she could in her photographs of what is still as it was in his time, while showing aspects of modern New England. In some instances she has had to search far and long to find the composition she wanted in a given area without having it include cast-off tires or other junk.

The topography and civic development, manners and morals, religion and education of each village or town he passed through became the pigments of Timothy Dwight's in-depth portrayal of New England for New Englanders, then and now.

They also reflect his own wide range of interests. The son of parents whose families had long records of intellectual and moral achievement in building New England, with roots especially in Massachusetts and Connecticut, Dwight had been a precocious child. He acquired knowledge at a phenomenally early age, was a Yale student at thirteen, and returned there as a tutor at the

*New Haven: S. Converse, 1821–1822.

age of twenty after two years of teaching elsewhere. He broke all precedents by marrying while still a tutor (Mary Woolsey, a girl from Long Island), and earned the antagonism of the college by being openly critical of its administration and independent of its protocol. The antagonism culminated in one final incident. Because of the war situation in 1776, the Yale Corporation had moved the senior class from New Haven to Wethersfield, Connecticut. They decreed that there would be no graduation ceremony that summer. Dwight ignored the decree, and he himself delivered a valedictory address, one which reflected nis own independence of spirit. He urged his students to think of themselves as citizens of the world. The Yale Corporation found his disobedience intolerable. It is not certain whether Dwight was forced to resign at this point or chose to, because of the Corporation's attitude, but his career at the college ended.

Dwight had confessed his faith and desire to enter the ministry in 1774, and he had become a student of his famous uncle, the Reverend Jonathan Edwards, Jr. Less than a year after his dismissal from Yale, in June 1777, he was approved for the Congregational ministry and was licensed to preach. Two years later, his father died suddenly. With his mother and eleven younger brothers and sisters as well as his own growing family dependent upon him, Dwight farmed his father's estate in Northampton, Massachusetts, for the next five years. He also established a small coeducational school which became very popular; in fact, it lured some students from Yale. He was active in local politics—as a member of the Massachusetts Legislature in 1781 and 1782—but preferred not to become involved in national politics though his friends urged him to become a delegate to the Continental Congress.

When a call came from the congregation at Greenfield Parish in Fairfield, Connecticut, for a preacher, he accepted the post gladly and was ordained in 1783.

For the next twelve years, Dwight played an important role in the ecumenical movement of his day. He had a more sanguine outlook upon man's relationship to God and the latter's patience with man than did many of his ancestors or contemporaries.

Resenting not only any criticism of the United States from abroad, but most particularly the influence of European thought upon young American minds, Dwight was an isolationist. He became a powerful speaker both inside and outside his church.

When President Stiles of Yale died in 1795, after seventeen brilliant years during which the college had become a one-man institution, the Corporation looked upon Timothy Dwight as his logical successor. His youthful indiscretions were forgotten.

Dwight accepted the call despite bitter opposition from his parish; for he believed that as president of Yale he could most stoutly fight the misconceptions, misinformation, and cynicism of Europe, and especially of Great Britain, in regard to the new nation. He decided that the best way to correct misconceptions, refute what he considered lies, and at the same time enlighten posterity was to spend his vacations investigating and noting the facts of geography, economy, and industry in New England. Between trips, he rounded out his notes and at the same time arranged the sequence of the journeys for publication. Upon his death, in 1817, his express wish was that the resulting four volumes of "letters" be published. They provide a remarkable firsthand study of a young civilization.

He wanted to know how New England would have appeared to him eighty or a hundred years before, but he soon found that information concerning this subject was chiefly unattainable: "A country changing as rapidly as New England must, if truly exhibited, be described in a manner resembling that in which a painter would depict a cloud," he writes. "The form and colors of the moment must be seized, or the picture will be erroneous. As it was naturally presumed by me that some of those who live eighty or a hundred years hence must have feelings similar to my own, I resolved to furnish, so far as should be in my power, means of enabling them to know what was the appearance of their country during the period occupied by my journeys."

Dwight's travels began in 1795, in the first year of his presidency, and continued for twenty years. He made four series of a few trips each, and incorporated each series into a volume of his *Travels in New-England and New-York*. His Volume I covered the four journeys he made from 1792 to 1802 and is here followed in Volume I. Similarly, this Volume II retraces his second volume, covering his five journeys taken from 1803 to 1815.

Volume I begins with Maine, and follows Dwight's trip from New Haven to Berwick. The pleasures of the coast, with sea and fog and rocks and the beautiful severities of winter, are here. In the next section, the journey is to New Hampshire, with emphasis on the White Mountains. Then he travels to Vergennes, Vermont, but with special attention to the charms of Connecticut. Finally, Massachusetts and Rhode Island, with their natural and historic riches, are captured, with the journey ending at Provincetown.

In Volume II, each of the major trips begins near the mouth of the Connecticut River. The first continues northward to its source, then travels overland to other rivers, taking Dwight to the Canada line. The next trip veers West, skirting the Green Mountains and making occasional excursions into New York across the western border of Vermont. Lake Champlain and its magnificent valley, with a Vermont shoreline of around one hundred and fifty miles, were the climax of the journey. (Although Dwight visited New York and described it at greater length in his later volumes, there are only small references to it in the earlier two.) The third trip is a return to Maine, but this time traveling up the coast of Maine to Portland and then on to Brunswick and Augusta. Last are two trips to beautiful Lake Winnipesaukee, the largest lake wholly contained within New England.

Dwight's travels took place at a time when America was engaged in strengthening her position as a nation, at the end of Washington's administration and during those of Adams, Jefferson, and Madison. In Europe, John Locke's ideas dominated the world of philosophy. While Beethoven and Haydn were composing their greatest music, folk songs and hymns were predominant in America. Her greatest painter, John Singleton Copley, had emigrated with several others to England, where they felt their work was appreciated more than in their native land. Except for a few itinerant primitives who painted village scenes, portraiture was the dominant theme in American art, and Gilbert Stuart, Charles Willson Peale, and Ralph Earl were its greatest urban exponents. The Hudson River School of landscape painting had not yet begun to show Americans the grandeur of the wilderness beyond their own doors, though novelists of the day sandwiched events in the lives of their protagonists between rhapsodic word-pictures of the scenery around them.

The major industries—aside from those activities, like farming, hunting, and fishing, which provided immediate sustenance in the outlands—were primarily coastal: shipbuilding, importing, and exporting. Eli Whitney had already invented his cotton gin, and Samuel Slater had arrived from England with an accurate blueprint in his brain of Richard Arkwright's cotton-cloth-producing machinery, which had been reproduced in mills at Providence, Rhode Island. But the Industrial Revolution was still far from being a factor in American life.

Some of Dwight's trips along the Connecticut River and east coast of Massachusetts were near repeats of previous ones and gave him the opportunity to observe progress or the lack of it over a considerable period of time. His third journey to Maine, for example, was made nearly ten years after the first two.

He not only made note therefore of the present state of affairs wherever he went, but added what data he could find from the past, as well as data on population and industry during subsequent visits or from later census reports or other reliable sources.

Dwight was profoundly convinced that the New England way of life presented a totally new concept to the whole world, and his *Travels* were made and documented to produce evidence of this.

The journeys are filled with incidents of enormous perseverance and extraordinary courage and endurance. The story of the settlers of Windsor, Connecticut, is typical of many:

"The hardships encountered by the first planters are not easily conceivable. . . ." Dwight notes. "These settlements you will remember were more than one hundred miles from any haunt of civilized man, and the journey lay through a wilderness hardly passable. Unhappily, they . . . arrived at the place of their destination a short time only before the approach of winter. Here they were obliged to encamp in the forest until they could furnish themselves with huts. They had shipped their furniture and provisions at Boston, and lost the principal part of both by shipwreck. They were, therefore, in a great measure destitute even of the necessaries of life and threatened with absolute famine. . . . Seventy of them embarked in a small vessel released from the ice by a copious rain, and after various misfortunes arrived safely at Boston. Those whom they left behind were by this diminution probably preserved from starving.

"During the first winter a great number of their cattle perished. . . . An ox, a cow, or a horse could be replaced from England only. They were encircled by savages whose good will was precarious and whose declaration of war was a massacre or a conflagration. Peace, safety, and life, therefore, hung perpetually in doubt; and suspense became a calamity scarcely inferior to those which were most dreaded. . . ."

In the mountainous areas of New England, settlers had to deal with a totally different set of problems before they could begin to clear the land. Riding along still difficult roads in the White Mountains, "a reflecting traveler . . ." Dwight comments, "is naturally induced to recollect the situation of the first colonists in New England. . . . Almost all the roads in which they traveled passed through deep forests and over rough hills and mountains, often over troublesome and dangerous streams, and not unfrequently through swamps, miry and hazardous, where wolves, bears, and catamounts haunted and alarmed their passage. The forests they could not cut down; the rocks they could not remove; the swamps they could not causey [by laying two large logs from one bank to the other and covering them with small logs laid transversely]; and over the streams they could not erect bridges. Men, women, and children ventured daily through this combination of evils, penetrated the recesses of the wilderness, climbed the hills, wound their way among the rocks, struggled through the mire, and swam on horseback through deep and rapid rivers by which they were sometimes carried away. To all these evils was added one more distressing than all. In the silence and solitude of the forest, the Indian often lurked in ambush near their path. . . .

"The settlement of a new country is an object which has not been hitherto described, I believe, by any writer. . . . To clear a farm covered with a thick growth of large trees such as generally abound in this country is a work of no small magnitude. Especially is this true when, as is usually the fact, it is to be done by a single man. . . . When a planter commences this undertaking, he sets out for his farm with his axe, gun, blanket, provision, and ammunition. With these he enters the forest and builds himself a shed by putting up poles at four angles, crossing them with other poles, and covering the whole with bark, leaves, and twigs of trees, except the south side, purposely left open to the sun and a fire. Under this shelter he dresses his food and makes his bed of straw, on which he sleeps soundly beneath his blanket. Here he usually continues through the season, and sometimes without the sight of any other human being. After he has completed this shelter, he begins to clear a spot of ground, i.e. to remove the forest by which it is covered. . . . The trees are cut down. . . . After they have lain a sufficient length of time, he sets fire to them, lying as they fell. If he is successful, the greater part of them are consumed in the conflagration. The remainder he cuts with his axe into pieces of a convenient length, rolls them into piles, and sets fire to them again. In this manner they are all consumed; and the soil is left light, dry, and covered with ashes. . . .

"After the field is burned over, his next business is to break it up. The instrument employed for this purpose is a large and strong harrow, here called a *drag*, with very stout iron teeth resembling in its form the capital letter A. It is drawn over the surface a sufficient number of times to make it mellow, and afterwards to cover the seed. A plow would here be of no use, as it would soon be broken to pieces by the roots of the trees. . . .

"The first house which he builds is formed of logs and commonly contains two rooms with a stone chimney in the middle. His next labor is to procure a barn, generally large, well framed, covered, and roofed. Compared with his house, it is a palace. But for this a sawmill is necessary and is therefore built as early as possible. . . .

"Every good planter who seats himself in a new township increases the value of every acre which it contains, because he induces other men to settle around him. Accordingly, the owners of large, unsettled tracts give several farms to individuals who are willing first to settle on them, that they may induce others to purchase the remainder. . . .

"These settlers . . . possess the energy which results from health, as well as that which results from activity; and few persons taste the pleasures which fall to their lot with a keener relish. The common troubles of life, often deeply felt by persons in easy circumstances, scarcely awaken in them the slightest emotion. Cold and heat, snow and rain, labor and fatigue are regarded by them as trifles deserving no attention. The coarsest food is pleasant to them, and the hardest bed refreshing. Over roads encumbered with rocks, mire, and the stumps and roots of trees, they ride upon a full trot, and are apprehensive of no danger. Even their horses gain by habit the same resolution, and pass rapidly and safely over the worst roads, where both horses and men accustomed to smoother ways merely tremble and creep."

The "grand divisions" of New England at the beginning of Dwight's journeys consisted of The District of Maine (it would not become a state until 1820), New Hampshire, Vermont, Massachusetts, Rhode Island, and Connecticut. The census of 1800 was only three years away, but parts of the area were still dense wilderness. The population per square mile at that time is interesting: "Maine about five . . . New Hampshire more than eighteen, Vermont fifteen, Massachusetts proper sixty-three, Rhode Island forty-six, Connecticut fifty." It was not essentially different ten years later, and it is still true that Maine has far fewer inhabitants per square mile than do the rest.

Timothy Dwight had some interesting comments about the men and women of New England: "The persons of the New Englanders," he writes, "their complexion, manners, and language, so much resemble those of Englishmen that the similarity has, as you know [Dwight is, as usual, writing to his imaginary correspondent], been the subject of not a little discussion on both sides of the Atlantic in the knotty case of impressing seamen. . . . Whether we are brave or cowardly, I will leave to be decided by the battles of Breed's Hill, Hoosick, Stillwater, and Saratoga, and by the attack on Stony Point. . . . We are said to be grave. Gravity is merely a comparative term. . . . The truth unquestionably is, our social meetings are probably as cheerful, sprightly, and replenished as often with sallies of wit and good humor as those of any other people. . . . It must be acknowledged that we think, converse, and write much less concerning theaters and actors than the inhabitants of London. . . . Amusements are not here the principal concern of life. . . . But whatever may be thought of the value of amusements, or of the nature of the stage, it is certain that the people of New England consider the former as of far less importance than the sober business of life, and the latter as having little claim to respect or even to indulgence. . . ."

Perhaps, even in Dwight's time, memory of the hazards of settlement and tales of Indian captivity were still too real for "made-up" drama to have much point. There are many such tales throughout these journeys as that of Mrs. Rowlandson, who was taken captive during a devastating raid upon Lancaster, Massachusetts. After assaulting the house of the Reverend Mr. Rowlandson, the minister, for two hours, the Indians "set it on fire, killed twelve persons, and took the rest prisoners. Mrs. Rowlandson was among the captives, together with one of her sisters and the children of both." She and her baby were wounded by the same musket ball.

"The next day they began their march. . . . From Wednesday night till Saturday night she had no other sustenance but water. By the advice of an English captive she put oak leaves upon her wound and obtained a cure. Nine days she held her child in her arms or upon her lap. During this time it had received nothing but cold water. At the close of the ninth day it expired and was buried by the Indians. She was then sold by the Narraganset Indian who took her captive to Quannopin, a Sagamore who married the sister of Philip's wife, a woman in whom Mrs. Rowlandson found a most uncomfortable mistress. . . .

"She was beaten, kicked, turned out of doors, refused food, insulted in the grossest manner, and at times almost starved. Nothing but experience can enable us to conceive what must be the hunger of a person by whom the discovery of six acorns and two chestnuts was regarded as a rich prize. At times, in order to make her miserable, they announced to her the death of her husband and her children. One of the savages, of whom she inquired concerning her son, told her that his master had, at a time which he specified, killed and roasted him, that himself had eaten a piece of him as big as his two fingers, and that it was delicious meat. On various occasions they threatened to kill her. Occasionally, but for short intervals only, she was permitted to see her children, and suffered her own anguish over again in their miseries. She was also obliged, while hardly able to walk, to carry a heavy burden over hills and through rivers, swamps, and marshes, and that in the most inclement seasons. . . . It is to be remembered that Mrs. Rowlandson was tenderly and delicately educated, and as ill-fitted to encounter these distresses as persons who have received such an education now are in this and other countries."

It is hard for us to imagine enduring what Mrs. Rowlandson and others endured in those times, yet it should not be too difficult, for the hazards of the wars of our time produce equally amazing stories of personal bravery. The difference is that these sufferings took place *here*—not in remote Far Eastern countrysides—in the civilizing of lands we in New England pass through every day with seldom a thought of how they were won.

Throughout his letters, Dwight reiterates over and over again his sound respect for the concept of democracy. "In the early part of this work," he writes, "I observed that every man in New England, almost without an exception, lives on his own ground, and that the lands are universally holden in fee simple, and by law descend to the children in equal shares. Elsewhere, I have observed also that every freeman is eligible to any office, and that a great proportion of them actually hold public offices at some time or other of their lives. . . . We have in New England no such class of men as on the eastern side of the Atlantic are denominated *peasantry*. . . . Here every apprentice originally intends to establish and, with scarcely an exception, actually establishes himself in business. Every seaman designs to become, and a great proportion of them really become, mates and masters of vessels; and every young man hired to work upon a farm aims steadily to acquire a farm for himself, and hardly one fails of the acquisition. We have few of those amphibious beings of whom you have such a host, who pass through life under the name of *journeymen*. All men here are masters of themselves, and such is the combined effect of education and society that he who fails of success in one kind of business may almost of course betake himself with advantage to another. . . . The means of comfortable living are in New England so abundant, and so easily obtained, as to be within the reach of every man who has health, industry, common honesty, and common sense."

In the last volume of his *Travels,* Dwight reminds his "correspondent" that it was his original intention to avoid reading accounts of America given by European travelers. "My reason was," he writes, "I wished to come to everything which I saw without any bias from the opinions of others, and to examine everything in the very light in which it should appear to *me.* At the same time I proposed to read, after I had examined for myself, what had been written by others, for the purpose both of renouncing my own errors and correcting theirs." He then systematically took exception to the testimonies of four European writers, Messrs. Volney and Weld, the Duke de La Rochefoucauld, and Mr. Lambert, who had traveled in the United States between 1795 and the early 1800s and had published accounts of their experiences.

He defends the language of New England. "It is no exaggeration to say that from Machias to St. Marys, and from the Atlantic to the Mississippi, every American descended from English ancestors understands every other as readily as if he had been bred in the same neighborhood," he writes; then gives a short but telling catalog of "elegant peculiarities" of the English language to be found in London alone.

Quoting the *Edinburgh Review* on Ashe's *Travels in America:* "In short, federal America has done nothing either to extend, diversify, or embellish the sphere of human knowledge. . . . The destruction of her whole literature would not occasion so much regret as we feel for the loss of a few leaves from an ancient classic," Dwight declares the statements untrue and goes on to explain why at some length. He describes the state of learning in America, principally in New England, and cites the achievements of individual men of the church, and of inventors such as Whitney and his cotton machine and David Bushnell, who, while still a student at Yale, invented the precursor to the modern submarine.

"To these things was added necessarily, the establishment of a government, a religion, a system of education, and universally a state of society," he continues, "by means of which the descendants of those on whom the burden rested might, so far as their circumstances would permit, be free, enlightened, virtuous, and happy. Occupied in this spacious and various field, the inhabitants have in few instances had either leisure or inclination to write books; and most of those which have been written were prompted by some particular occasion.

"Let me request you to remember how long your own nation existed before it could boast of a single well-written book. In the eighth century you had only the venerable Bede; in the ninth, only Alfred; in the tenth and eleventh, none; in the twelfth, William of Malmesbury is entitled to respect. Roger Bacon adorned the thirteenth. From that time till the sixteenth you had no writer of any distinction except Fortescue, Chaucer, and Gower. In the sixteenth century, you number only five or six writers of respectability. The seventeenth and eighteenth have filled your hemisphere with constellations. Before Hume and Robertson, you had no historian superior to several of ours. The reviewer is disposed to speak contemptuously of Marshall's Life of Washington. Yet there is no piece of biography written in Great Britain, if we except those of Johnson, which would not suffer by a comparison with it."

In his final letter, Timothy Dwight speaks again of the conversion of America from "an immense wilderness into a fruitful field"—which, to him, only a God-loving, peaceful, free people could have created: "I think you will agree that no such scene has hitherto been presented to the eye of men as that which the American States may be justly said to exhibit." To the possible objection of his correspondent that the States might soon be dissevered into separate empires that would be at war with one another, Dwight's reply was one of hope and belief that even if such disaster should occur, his beloved New England and New York would be united in the same political body and would find together "peculiar sources of national greatness and prosperity."

Dwight describes the contours of New England, the sweep of its mountain ranges, its rivers and harbors, as though he had the whole of it under his fingertips.

"I have often lamented," he writes, "that I had not received an early education in mineralogy and botany, but never so much as since I began the series of journeys which have given birth to these observations. . . . I shall, therefore, present you sketches, rather than regular details." But his "sketches" are amazingly informative. We are given data on soil strata, rock formations, forest tree varieties (over sixty, each with some detail of its appearance and usefulness); fruit trees, shrubs, and vines (at least twenty species of apples, the russets and the greenings and the pippins, and the intriguingly named "Early Seek No Further" and "Late Seek No Further" among them); flowering shrubs; some fifty different vegetables, and seventeen kinds of produce; animals, fish, insects and their ravages; varieties in climate, wind patterns and their cause; and the history of the most remarkable tempests and droughts.

After the frequent thunderstorms, "the earth, particularly in the months of May and June, the richest season of vegetation, is beautiful beyond description," he declares. "The verdure glows with new life, the flowers exult with additional beauty and fragrance;

> 'The birds their notes renew; and bleating herds
> Attest their joy, that hill and valley rings.' "*

Beneath the encyclopedist and the statistician, one becomes aware of the inner softness of this rather crusty individual. He really did *love* New England, and the increasing knowledge his travels brought him only deepened that love.

Dwight's later travels encompassed the War of 1812, its prologue and its aftermath. One would think that Timothy Dwight, who made inflammatory sermons against every aspect of the war, would have expressed his Federalist sympathies in his study of New England. Amazingly, his meticulous and encyclopedic records include scarcely any direct reference to the Federalists, either during the war buildup or its actuality.

Perhaps Dwight deliberately abstained from any comment on the war because he feared the subject was so emotional that it would overshadow his chosen task. He believed the informative mosaic he was putting together, town by town, had more relevance for the future than did the

*Milton's *Paradise Lost*

War of 1812. The creation of a civilization by people who had left their own countries to build a place in a wilderness because there they could follow their own way of life was of far deeper significance than the war that could only interrupt that process.

One cannot read Dwight's Preface nor the fourteen letters that precede the actual start of his journey to Berwick without considering him, by his own definition, a member of the curious rather than incurious among men. "Persons of the latter class," he writes, "busy themselves only with general principles.... Their descriptions resemble the last impressions of a copperplate, when the lines are so worn out as to be scarcely distinguishable. . . . Persons of the former class . . . early learn that general views, although useful for arranging and teaching the objects of science, are of little use to an inquirer except in their application, in which they of course become particular. . . ."

Early in his narrative he defines some of the terms he uses: "*town*, in the language of New England, denotes a collection of houses in the first parish, if the township contains more than one, constituting the principal, and ordinarily the original, settlement in that parish. A *street* is the way on which such a collection of houses is built, but does not at all include the fact that the way is paved. . . . A great part of the streets in New England, exclusively of the paths which run through them, are, during the pleasant season, equally verdant with the neighboring fields. . . ." By *interval* Dwight means "lands formed by a long continued and gradual alluvion of a river"—lands which in states south of New England would be called *flats* and *bottoms*. "From the manner in which these lands were brought into existence, we shall easily believe that they are of the richest quality. Such is almost invariably the fact. . . . Nor are these grounds less distinguished by their beauty. The form of most of them is elegant. . . .

"The attachment felt by every man to the land which gave him birth, and which invests it in his mind with a peculiar importance, will be rationally supposed to have enhanced these considerations in my own," he concludes. "If a Laplander believes the frosty region around him to have been the seat of Paradise, and an Icelander can find a comfortable life nowhere but in the dreary island in which he was born, it cannot be thought strange that a native of New England should feel a part of the same interest in the scenes which have accumulated so many and so various enjoyments around himself and all who have been dear to him from his earliest remembrance."

Thus stoutly does Timothy Dwight defend his yearly odysseys and their object.

Volume I

MAINE

Wilderness landscape, Baxter State Park

Opposite: *Forest road in Baxter State Park, Maine*

Pemaquid Point Light, warning vessels of forbidding rocks

Opposite: *Logging booms on the Penobscot River*

Lobsterman baiting his traps on the Maine coast

Rocks and surf, New Harbor

Summer cruising off Boothbay in a windjammer

The town and harbor of Stonington, Deer Isle

Morning fog from a Rockland wharf

Journey to Berwick

WHAT can be more of a contrast than the mysterious far-north reaches of Baxter State Park and the gentle closeness of small villages clustered and blooming under the sun along Maine's coast? What can be more beautiful than her mountains and valleys, what more sudden and abrupt and at the same time subtle than her movement from season to season? In Maine you do not expect a gradual approach of spring, you are suddenly aware of its delicate and evanescent presence. Sea and fog and sparkling light, blue sky and autumn fire—these are Maine.

The Indians knew these joys long before the settlers came.

Over and over, Timothy Dwight points out the peculiar difficulties encountered by builders of New England settlements. The greatest of these was the uncertainty of their relationship with the Indians. Seven wars were fought from 1675, when King Philip's War began, through the year 1783. The first was a futile attempt on the part of the Indians themselves to unite and drive the intruders out. Five of the wars were instigated by the French and the last one by the British during the Revolutionary War.

Even where colonists and their Indian neighbors had been coexisting peacefully, a man might return from working in his fields to find his home burned down and his family murdered, or no one there to greet him. His imagination would furnish ample detail of his wife and children being pushed and prodded along wooded or rocky paths toward a life of slavery in Indian wigwams or far north in Canada.

In addition, the coast of Maine took a beating during the Revolutionary War, when British sloops could turn their guns on helpless towns from a distance, as happened to Falmouth (now Portland) on October 18, 1775. "All the public buildings except the Congregational church, one hundred and thirty dwelling houses, and a great number of outbuildings" were reduced to ashes, and 160 families were driven "to find an asylum from the winter in the country thinly inhabited," Dwight reports.

At the time of his first recorded journey in 1796, the more remote villages of Maine had been free of the constant fear of Indian attack for only twelve years.

Dwight describes the state as being in general colder than any other, "but not so cold as to prevent mankind when possessed of even moderate property from passing through the year comfortably and cheerfully. . . . In the southwestern parts are extensive plains. Farther eastward and northward, the surface is to a great extent formed into hills and valleys. . . . Maine is everywhere intersected by brooks and rivers. . . . The waters throughout are pure and salubrious [today, awakened Mainers would dispute this statement, for many of her rivers and lakes run stagnant and have lost their sweetness]. . . . Both the rivers, and the sea which washes this coast, abound with fish of excellent kinds in quantities inexhaustible. . . . Upon the whole, it will be no immoderate calculation to suppose that, with its advantages for agriculture, fishing, and commerce, Maine may hereafter easily support from four to five millions of people."

Undoubtedly Dwight is correct as far as what Maine *could* do—more and more out-of-staters are reaching the same conclusion at the present time. But his prophecy as far as population is concerned is way beyond the mark. In 1960 the population reached 969,000, and in 1970, it only just passed the million mark.

Dwight believed Maine remained so sparsely settled because commerce and fishing were the motivating forces for its settlers, rather than the hope of civil or religious freedom: "Men . . . influenced by some great and commanding motive . . . are the only persons fitted to subdue forests, encounter frost and hunger, and resolutely survey the prospect of savage incursions. . . . From the first settlers of Maine . . . all that could be rationally expected was that which actually took place. They traded, caught fish, and went home."

People who seek refuge in Maine today are still not motivated by the hope of civil or religious freedom—though actually, the relative sparseness of its settlement does make room for tolerance. Many—especially among younger people—who come here now, come in search of salvation from the nonpersonal, artificial, harried existence of metropolitan cities. They come in search of clean air and water, of far clear skies and tall trees; of people who respect you for what you are, not how much you own; of time to be quiet, to look, to listen, to gather and enjoy the fruits of the earth and the sea.

The springboard of all Dwight's journeys was, of course, Connecticut. Though he was born in Massachusetts (May 14, 1752), once he moved his family to the parsonage in Fairfield, the state of Connecticut became his home, and he died January 11, 1817, at New Haven.

After a brief factual description of that state, Dwight analyzes New Haven in really extraordinary detail before setting down the record of his first journey. The soil texture of the plain on which the city is built; the marsh mud, which was then closing up the harbor at the head of which the city lay; the three rivers whose confluence created the harbor; the hills and the valleys that ornamented the landscape; the layout of New Haven streets, its architecture, its churches—all come under his scrutiny. He carefully lists fifty-six occupational activities by number, from "29 houses concerned in foreign commerce" to "9 practicing physicians and 1 surgeon," because the list "exhibits more perfectly . . . the state of society in an American town than it would be possible to derive from any other source." He gives New Haven's population; the dollar amount and tonnage of its imports and exports, foreign and domestic; the price of labor (a dollar a day in 1810, when he was writing most of his prefatory material), and of foods, starting with seven to ten cents a pound for the better cuts of beef.

No future historian of the city, it seems to us, could approach the subject without taking cognizance of the material Timothy Dwight's "curiosity" provided in Letters XV and XVI of the Journey to Berwick, which began on Wednesday, September 21, 1796.

Archway glimpse of Yale University Campus

Dwight's discourse on New Haven included the history of the establishment and progress of Yale College, a description of its studies for an average of 260 students at thirty-three dollars tuition per year, and considerable detail as to its government. As he remarks to his imaginary correspondent, "From the office which I hold in it, you may fairly regard the story as claiming your confidence." From the first wooden building of 1717–18, three colleges of stone, a chapel, and a lyceum had evolved by the time Dwight was writing.

The city of Hartford, Dwight found, boasted better buildings than those in New Haven. No doubt this was due to the fact that the inhabitants by a public vote had forbidden the construction of wooden houses within the compact part of their city—the only people in Connecticut to do this. "Posterity will have reason to remember this measure with gratitude," Dwight believed. His description of the State House with its "Doric portico, thirty feet high, of ten columns, built of brick, and stuccoed white," includes actual measurements of inside rooms as well as of the outward structure. One cannot help wondering, after reading the encyclopedic information Dwight gives about buildings, bridges, canals, locks, how he managed to amass all the facts. But if one thing is certain, those facts had to be accurate—one cannot imagine that Dwight would have been guilty of stating anything at any time that he did not have reason to believe was absolutely true.

Old State House, Hartford, Connecticut, built 1796

Since Hartford was already the seat of government in Connecticut, Dwight digressed into a detailed discussion of the state's handling of the law, before proceeding with a description of the intervals and the towns on the Connecticut River they rode through on the third day of their journey, from Hartford to Springfield. "The people of Windsor, like some others on this river," he wrote, "appear to have adopted a regular, but easy, industry, and to have formed a settled character which seems unlikely to be soon changed by their descendants"—who now carefully cultivate tobacco in their still-rich meadows.

Tobacco plants at Windsor, Connecticut

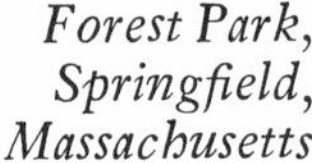

Forest Park, Springfield, Massachusetts

Intervals along the Connecticut River as seen from Mt. Tom, near Holyoke, Massachusetts

"... The most exquisite scenery of the whole landscape is formed by the river and its extended margin of beautiful intervals . . . fields containing from five hundred to five thousand acres, formed like terraced gardens. . . ."

Verdant Main Street, in Hadley, Massachusetts, town's oldest house in foreground

A farm scene in Brookfield, Massachusetts

"The hills are high; and the valleys, particularly along the river Quaboag, deep," Dwight wrote, "wild, solitary, and not a little romantic." In its passage through Brookfield, the river "is a remarkably sluggish stream. . . . Yet the inhabitants are distinguished for health and longevity. A number of persons have died here who were about one hundred years of age. Mrs. Elizabeth Olds, who died in her ninety-second year, had ten children, seventy-three grandchildren, 201 great grand-children, and two of the fourth generation: in all 286, 232 of whom were living at her decease."

The Quaboag River, wild and solitary

"On the subject of *mills* I wish you to observe, once for all, that I shall rarely mention them," Dwight promised while taking account of those in Worcester. "A New Englander cannot refrain from smiling" when a town is described as fortunate in having two mills, he went on. "There is probably no country in the world" where gristmills and sawmills are "so universally erected as in New England. . . . To reiterate this fact would be . . . very effectual means for wearing out your patience." In Dwight's time, Worcester also boasted three printing offices, the proprietor of one of them being Isaiah Thomas, official printer for Massachusetts Bay's patriots and founder of the American Antiquarian Society.

Rooftops in Worcester, Massachusetts

Concord River scene, North Bridge in the background, Concord, Massachusetts

On October 1, Dwight and his companion rode thirty-six miles from Marlboro to Andover, lingering at Concord on the way, which town, he wrote, "will be long remembered as having been, partially, the scene of the first military action in the Revolutionary War, and the object of an expedition, the first in that chain of events which terminated in the separation of the British colonies from their mother country. . . . From the plains of Concord will henceforth be dated a change in human affairs, an alteration in the balance of human power, and a new direction to the course of human improvement. . . ."

Now tourists walk where Thoreau walked, muse over his brand of independence, and visit the Hancock-Clarke House, where John Hancock and Samuel Adams, each afterward governor of Massachusetts, were guests and supposedly the objects also of the British expedition sent to destroy military stores at Concord. They were warned in time to escape, by Colonel Paul Revere, official courier for the Massachusetts Provincial Assembly, and Mr. William Dawes, who rode with him. Both were stopped by the British before they reached Concord, but a young Dr. Prescott, to whom they had given the alarm, escaped and was able to warn the township in time.

Wooded path along Walden Pond, in Concord

The British troops, having failed to find the principal stores at Concord and been forced to retreat at the Battle of North Bridge, "were continually harassed by an irregular and not ill-directed fire from the buildings and walls" on their way to Lexington. "Every moment increased the number of their assailants and their own fatigue, distress, and danger," Dwight recounted. "Upon the first intelligence that the Americans had betaken themselves to arms," a second detachment of nine hundred men was added to the Concord expedition. They "marched from Boston with two fieldpieces, their music playing the tune of Yankee Doodle to insult the Americans." But after they joined the forces at Lexington, they were employed in covering their retreat rather than joining them in attack. "Everywhere the retreating army was pursued and flanked. Their enemies descended from every new hill and poured through every new valley. . . ."

Left: *The Lexington Minute Man, Lexington, Massachusetts*

Below: *Interior, Hancock-Clarke House, Lexington, built 1698*

From Concord Dwight and his companion traveled through the Billerica and Tewksbury area, where may still be seen the remains of the Middlesex Canal, completed in 1801, "the most considerable work of the kind in the United States. Its length is near thirty miles from Charles River to the Merrimack. To the Merrimack it descends from Concord River, in five miles and three quarters, twenty-one feet; and from Concord to Charles River, through the remaining distance, 107 feet. The former of these descents is compassed by means of three locks, the latter by means of thirteen. The design of forming this canal was to introduce from the countries on the Merrimack and its headwaters into Boston the great quantities of timber and the artificial produce which they furnish. . . ."

Remains of Middlesex Canal Aqueduct that crossed the Shawsheen River

Fall shadows on Main Street, Billerica, Massachusetts

"The town of Billerica stands on a pretty eminence, easily ascended and of considerable height, presenting to the eye an extensive prospect of the neighboring country," Dwight wrote. "The manners of the plain inhabitants appear, like many of their houses, to retain in an uncommon degree the ancient simplicity of New England."

The scheme of Phillips Academy, founded April 1, 1778, "was formed by the Hon. Samuel Phillips, late lieutenant governor of Massachusetts, when only twenty-one years of age," Dwight wrote. "By his solicitations, his father and uncle gave the extensive benefactions which founded both the academies at Andover and Exeter. Of this property, he was the natural and presumptive heir. He was an only son; and his uncle, who had no child, regarded him with parental affection. In an important sense, therefore, the property thus given was all his own." It was Samuel's own son John and Samuel's widow Phoebe who undertook the responsibility of building the Andover Theological Seminary, which furthered the intent of Samuel's original bequest.

Phillips Andover Academy, Andover, Massachusetts, with Paul Manship's armillary sphere in foreground

Stevens Pond from Weir Hill, North Andover

Hay rick, North Andover farm landscape

"North Andover is a very beautiful piece of ground," Dwight observed. "Its surface is elegantly undulating, and its soil in an eminent degree fertile. The meadows are numerous, large, and of the first quality. The groves, charmingly interspersed, are tall and thrifty. The landscape, everywhere varied, neat, and cheerful, is also everywhere rich. . . ."

North Andover farm, winter snow

The travelers were on their way now from Andover to Haverhill, founded in 1637, and the scene of the Indian attack upon the Dustin family, March 5, 1697. The father, forced to leave his wife and newborn baby and her nurse behind, and, unable to choose which one of his seven children to save, stood his ground and defended their escape fiercely and successfully. The story that follows, of the murder of the baby and sufferings of Mrs. Dustin and the nurse on a 150-mile march is harrowing, typical of many that Dwight recorded in these journeys. But the ending was unusual. The threat of what would happen on arrival at their destination made the women desperate. "On the 31st... very early in the morning, Mrs. Dustin, while the Indians were asleep, having awakened her nurse and a fellow prisoner (a youth taken some time before from Worcester), dispatched, with the assistance of her companions, ten of the twelve Indians. The other two escaped. With the scalps of these savages, they returned through the wilderness...."

Wellsweep at Whittier's birthplace, built 1668, Haverhill, Massachusetts

Spring plowing, Merrimack Valley, Massachusetts

Looking across the Merrimack from Ward Hill to Haverhill

Great Bay, Portsmouth, New Hampshire

Somersworth, New Hampshire, across Salmon Falls River, from Berwick, Maine

The last lap of this journey crossed the Piscataqua River to a "rude, wild, and solitary" shore, by a bridge which Dwight likened to a well-contrived portrait "surrounded by such objects as leave the eye to rest on the principal one, and the mind to feel but a single impression."

The town of Berwick seen from Somersworth rooftops

From the bridge the travelers went through undulating country "of a cold soil," to Dover, and thence to Somersworth and across the Salmon Falls River to Berwick, the first settlement in the District of Maine. They had intended to go on to Portland, but found the road too bad for safe travel. However, they did ride to a spot in Sanford—and it must have been a very clear, sparkling Maine day—where they could get a view of Mount Washington, the highest peak of the White Mountains.

Opposite: *Quiet street in Strawbery Banke, Portsmouth, New Hampshire*

ATKINSON ST.

Portsmouth, the only seaport on New Hampshire's brief coast, "is built on a beautiful peninsula," Dwight observed, "on the south side of Piscataqua River, united with the main land by a narrow isthmus on the northwest, and by a bridge over a small inlet on the south. . . . As seen from the towers of the steeples, the opposite shore of Kittery, the river, the harbor, the ocean, the points, the islands, the town, and the adjacent country form a delightful assemblage of objects. . . ."

Portsmouth waterfront

Along Court Street, Portsmouth

Dwight was impressed by the favorable location of the town: "From the peculiar advantages of its situation, Portsmouth appears almost wholly to have escaped the ravages of the Indians. Secured on three sides by the Piscataqua, the ocean, and the inlet heretofore mentioned, it was accessible to savages only by the isthmus which connects it with the main. . . ." But he disapproved highly of the preponderance of wooden buildings in close contiguity, inviting destruction by fire; and though he found a few of the streets wide and pleasant, the town had been, in his opinion, "laid out without any regard to regularity."

About Newburyport, however, though he wished it had been laid out with a little more care also, Dwight was unstinting in his praise. "It lies on the southern shore of the Merrimack. The town is built on a declivity of unrivaled beauty. The slope is easy and elegant; the soil rich; the streets, except one near the water, clean and sweet; and the verdure, wherever it is visible, exquisite. . . . The houses taken collectively make a better appearance than those of any other town in New England."

High Street, Newburyport, Massachusetts

Whipple House, Ipswich, Massachusetts

"Ipswich is an ancient town, incorporated in 1634, and settled the next in this country after Salem. . . . The soil is good. The town is large, and the remaining part of the township, except an extensive salt marsh, is occupied by farms," Dwight reported. Though woolens and silk and thread lace were produced in Ipswich, the town seemed to be dying out, losing more citizens in the past ten years than Dwight had observed anywhere else.

A street in the town of Ipswich

By October 13 the travelers arrived at Salem, settled in 1626 by Roger Conant and his companions, "the oldest town in Massachusetts except Plymouth, and the largest except Boston," Dwight remarked. "It is built on a handsome peninsula of a level and very neat surface between Bass and South Rivers."

Kitson's statue of Roger Conant, Salem

Replica of typical Puritan hut, Pioneer Village, Salem, Massachusetts

In Dwight's time Salem included Danvers, which was anciently called Salem Village. It was here that the supposed prevalence of witchcraft resulted in the hysterical persecutions of 1692. Years before, the subject of witchcraft had flared up in Boston at a time when a wave of it had spread across Europe and England. In Salem it reached a higher peak than anywhere else in America. "Suspense and terror spread through the colony," Dwight reported. "Neither age nor sex, neither ignorance nor innocence, neither learning nor piety, neither reputation nor office furnished the least security" if one were accused, no matter by whom.

"As a commercial town, Salem ranks next to Charleston, South Carolina, being the sixth in the United States," Dwight reported. "It is also the sixth in population. In wealth proportioned to the number of its inhabitants, it is the first. The commerce of this town coastwise, with the West Indies, with Europe, with Africa, with India, and with China is carried on with an industry, enterprise, and skill highly honorable to the inhabitants, and has been attended with unrivaled success.

"The harbor, however, in which all this business is transacted is ill fitted for commercial enterprise. All vessels drawing more than twelve feet of water must be unladen at a distance from the town by lighters, and the wharves at low water are left dry."

The old Custom House, built in 1819, and Derby Wharf, Salem

The harbor at Marblehead, Massachusetts

Marblehead, next on their itinerary, Dwight found still suffering from the effects of the Revolutionary War. "The town made a better appearance to my eye in 1774 than in 1796," he wrote, which leads one to believe he had spent time there as a boy. The fishermen "labor hard in a very toilsome occupation, and frolic away the remembrance of their hardships during the winter."

The State House, Boston, designed by Charles Bulfinch, built 1795

Boston was the fulsome subject of Dwight's pen after a day spent there: its public buildings, bridges, and schools; its government and commerce and manufacturing; and finally the character of its people and what he called "their fashionable education," by which children soon "learn that the primary end of their efforts, and even of their existence, is *appearance only*. *What they are*, they soon discern is of little consequence; but, *what they appear to be* is of importance inestimable. The whole force of the early mind is directed, therefore, to this object, and exhausted in acquiring the trifles of which it is composed."

Park Street, Boston, on a snow-swept day

Boston's skyline, seen from across the Charles River at Cambridge

Writing of Harvard College, begun in the year 1636, only five years after the settlement of Cambridge was begun, and about which he had written earlier, in detail, Dwight observed: "I ought to have mentioned that the greatest disadvantage under which this seminary labors is the proximity of Boston. The allurements of this metropolis have often become too powerfully seductive to be resisted by the gay, and sometimes even by the grave youths who assemble here for their education."

It was in Cambridge that the "first printing office in New England was set up... at the expense of the Rev. Josse Glover, a clergyman who died on his passage to America.... The first thing printed in New England was the Freeman's Oath; the second, Pierce's New England Almanac; the third, the New England Version of the Psalms."

Rowing on the Charles River

Street scene, Providence, Rhode Island, State House in the background

Going through the suburbs of Boston and towns now bypassed by highways, the travelers found Carver "a lean looking collection of thinly scattered plantations"; Middleboro "destitute of beauty"; Taunton "much more sprightly and agreeable"; and finally toward Providence, the last four miles "intolerably bad, being a deep sand, very heavy, and most uncomfortably set with stones of a considerable size." Of North Providence, served by the Pawtucket River falls with power for millseats, Dwight wrote: "There is probably no spot in New England of the same extent in which the same quantity or variety of manufacturing business is carried on." He listed nineteen manufacturing concerns, plus several forges for smiths' work, as being active in 1796.

Benefit Street, Providence

Of Providence itself Dwight remarked that its morals were "probably superior to those of any other town in this state," but of the houses and roads surrounding it, he makes frequent use of the word "lean." Only when they reached Sterling, on the border of Connecticut, did welcome sights of fertile tracts and neat, cheery New England villages meet their eyes again.

They continued their homeward trip along the Quinebaug and Thames rivers, to New London, Saybrook, and finally New Haven, stopping only to visit the Mohegan Indian reservation at Montville and the spot where Uncas, their sachem, always friendly to the colonists, had lived.

NEW HAMPSHIRE

New Hampshire pines laced with winter snow

Opposite: *Lake Chocorua, with Mt. Chocorua in the background*

Passaconaway Bridge over the Swift River, Albany, New Hampshire

Summer landscape, valley of the White Mountains, Jackson

Lobster boats anchored in the Piscataqua River, Portsmouth

Street scene in old Charlestown, New Hampshire

The Saco River, below Crawford Notch, White Mountains in the distance

Journey to the White Mountains

HAVING failed to reach Portland, Maine, on his first journey, Dwight made this the goal of his second, but chose a route leading through "the Notch of the White Mountains" in New Hampshire—the only road which at that time led from the west to Portland. This time, he traveled with a tutor from Yale.

He found it difficult to divide the state of New Hampshire into neat sections that he could analyze. "The country along the Connecticut until we ascend the mountains of Littleton resembles that in Massachusetts. The valley, however, is generally narrower. . . ." he comments. "Much of it is better fitted for grazing than for agriculture. A great multitude of neat cattle fed in the pastures of New Hampshire are annually driven to the market on the eastern shore. To sheep a great part of the country is very well suited, and their numbers are fast increasing. . . . Few countries in the world are better furnished with millstreams and mill seats than New Hampshire.

"The proper New England character is, I think, more evident than in Vermont," he writes. "The political constitution is altogether better. . . ." But he found "a want of union and concern in the management of public affairs," probably due, as he points out, to the fact that a large number of the people of New Hampshire were lately immigrants from other states.

He found a different quality in their settlements. Those in states farther south and east had to be ready to face Indian attack, and the villages were built with that as a constant in mind. But most of New Hampshire was settled after the Peace of Paris (1763)—often by families who had suffered the ravages of Indian attack. They preferred the hardships and loneliness of striking root in the interior, and sought inaccessible places that could be defended like fortresses.

In one instance the travelers' host was reached after a perilous ascent up rocky paths of the Littleton Mountains some fourteen miles above Lancaster. The innkeeper was absent. Dwight's companion, feeling ill, went to bed supperless, but Dwight found himself a meal of partridge and coffee, "an entertainment which I had hardly expected in a house just built in an almost impenetrable forest," he comments. Five years before, the innkeeper had set out in the winter on an ox sled with his wife and child, to seek his fortune.

Dwight's friend Captain Eleazer Rosebrook had built a house in the Crawford Notch area. He had stationed himself in a wilderness twenty miles from his nearest neighbor, "subdued a farm of 150, or 200 acres, and built two large barns, the very boards of which he must have transported from a great distance with such expense and difficulty as the inhabitants of older settlements would think intolerable."

Perhaps the cacophonic splendor of the mountains and the great Notch itself, which to Timothy Dwight seemed the product of "some vast convulsion of nature," unquestionably "that of the deluge," put pressure upon a mere human to accomplish the tasks of a giant.

The Journey to the awesome White Mountains began September 18, 1797.

Old Deerfield house doorway

The travelers followed the Connecticut River in a beeline for New Hampshire, going through North Haven, Wallingford, Meriden, to Berlin (center for the tinware that toppled on peddlers' wagons in "every inhabited part of the United States") and on through a succession of small villages. Long before they reached the White Mountains, single mounts provided spectacular scenes along the river. It was from these heights that settlers were spied upon while they planted their fields, and from these heights that they were attacked when most vulnerable. In the Deerfield area, King Philip succeeded in uniting his countrymen into general war against the colonists. "Twice deserted, in 1675 and in 1677" because of Indian attack, Dwight reported, Deerfield was resettled in 1682, but in 1704 the town was set afire, "forty of the inhabitants were killed, and more than one hundred taken prisoners, amounting to one half of their whole number." Then, at what is now known as Bloody Brook, a company of soldiers, sent to protect Deerfield farmers who had come back to harvest wheat that had not been destroyed with the town, were slaughtered. Such a massacre, "unattended with that complication and confusion which envelop the horrors of regular war and hide its miseries from the eye, was sufficiently limited," Dwight observed, "to be comprehended by every mind, and sufficiently particular to be felt by every heart."

Opposite: *The main street in Old Deerfield, Massachusetts*

Walpole, New Hampshire

"Winding along the margin of one of the most beautiful and vivid intervals in New England," the travelers ascended a slope on the borders of Green River to Greenfield and then on through Walpole. North of this village were the dramatic Bellows Falls. A turnpike road from Boston passed through Walpole and crossed the river there. "As this is the principal channel of communication between Boston and the country on the northwest," Dwight took note, "the traveling and transportation on it are great. From these circumstances, this village has become the seat of considerable business. It contains a printing office and a bookstore."

Opposite: *The Connecticut River, looking toward Bellows Falls, Vermont*

A cloudscape taken near Ascutney, Vermont

"*Ascutney*, it is said, signifies *the three brothers* . . . to indicate the three principal summits of this mountain. . . ." Dwight wrote. "Clouds usually envelop the summit of Ascutney for some time before a rain, and rain commonly commences on the mountain before it descends on the subjacent country."

When Dwight and his companion reached Cornish, they were traveling through prosperous farmlands, in a different atmosphere from that of towns to the south, where lands and people still bore scars of past terror. "When we left Charlestown," Dwight commented, "we quitted the ground which was formerly the scene of Indian ravages. All the country above this town in New Hampshire and above Brattleboro in Vermont was almost an absolute wilderness until after the Peace of Paris. . . . After that time, the whole region was converted into a fruitful field with a rapidity which has rarely been paralleled."

Covered bridge between Cornish, New Hampshire, and Windsor, Vermont

Looking across the Connecticut River to Vermont from a point between Hanover and Lyme, both in New Hampshire

Passing through Dartmouth (at which point in his narrative Dwight provided a detailed history of the college), they headed through Lyme, Orford, Piermont, and Haverhill for Lancaster, on a road that "for a country so newly settled was good. . . . The journey was pleasant and romantic, the river, bordered in several places by small intervals, being frequently in sight and forming a cheerful contrast to the solemnity of the forest."

Crawford Notch in New Hampshire, the pass Indians used in marching prisoners north

One of the notable "Tory Row" houses built at Orford, New Hampshire, between 1773 and 1839

It is difficult to follow the exact itinerary of Dwight and his companion once they entered the White Mountains, for some of Dwight's name references do not jibe with present map locations. For example, he speaks of "the Flume" within half a mile of the gorgeous cascade he christened the Silver Cascades, in the Crawford Notch area. Today, another flume some ten miles away in the Franconia Notch is the tourist attraction.

They had left the Connecticut Valley and entered that of the Lower Ammonoosuc, and Dwight was almost overwhelmed by the majestic grandeur of the mountain slopes and peaks. Towering above the rest was Mount Washington. Dwight had seen its misty summit from some ninety miles away in Sanford, Maine. Looking back upon it and the other mountains of the range—this time from Hiram, half that distance—they saw "a long range of proud eminences, the loftier of which, covered with snow, majestically and gradually declined from the sight. In the center, Mount Washington, white and glittering, alternated with strong dark shadows, looked down upon these mountains as they did upon the world beneath. On the highest point rested a cloud, wild and tumultuous." From Conway, looking back up the mountains, "all the nearer and lower summits were blue and misty. But Mount Washington, illumined by the eastern sun, shone with a glittering white, having been covered with snow by the tempest of the preceding day. The deep shadows cast by the projecting cliffs enhanced the luster. On the highest point awfully brooded a cloud, tossed into wild and fantastical forms, and seemed to be the connecting link between the earth and the heavens."

Mt. Washington, in New Hampshire, highest in the Northeast

Franconia Notch, Mt. Lafayette in the distance

"When we entered the notch we were struck with the wild and solemn appearance of everything before us. . ." Dwight wrote. "The rocks, rude and ragged in a manner rarely paralleled, were fashioned and piled on each other by a hand operating only in the boldest and most irregular manner. As we advanced, these appearances increased rapidly. Huge masses of granite, of every abrupt form, and hoary with a moss which seemed the product of ages . . . speedily rose to a mountainous height. Before us, the view widened fast to the southeast. Behind us, it closed almost instantaneously, and presented nothing to the eye but an impassible (sic) barrier of mountains."

Opposite: *Skiing down Cannon Mountain, in the Franconia Notch*

The travelers "saw in full view the most beautiful cascade perhaps in the world. It issued from a mountain on the right, about eight hundred feet above the subjacent valley, and at the distance of about two miles from us. The stream ran over a series of rocks almost perpendicular, with a course so little broken as to preserve the appearance of an uniform current, and yet so far disturbed as to be perfectly white. The sun shone with the clearest splendor from a station in the heavens, the most advantageous to our prospect; and the cascade glittered down the vast steep like a stream of burnished silver."

"Silver Cascades" waterfall, christened by Timothy Dwight

Mt. Washington Valley, North Conway

"Wide and deep chasms also at times met the eye, both on the summits and the sides . . . hoary cliffs, rising with proud supremacy, frowned awfully on the world below and finished the landscape."

Ferns and forest trees, Pinkham Notch, New Hampshire

"As the eye ascended these steeps, the light decayed and gradually ceased. On the inferior summits rose crowns of conical firs and spruces. On the superior eminences, the trees, growing less and less, yielded to the chilling atmosphere, and marked the limit of forest vegetation. Above, the surface was covered with a mass of shrubs, terminating at a still higher elevation in a shroud of dark colored moss."

On the way to the village of Standish, Maine (below), *Dwight saw the great bend in the Saco River* (overleaf) *near Bartlett, New Hampshire*

Dwight and his companion left Conway on October 5 and rode forty-two miles to Standish, Fryeburg being the only town on their way and "the first in the District of Maine. The township," Dwight

observed, “lies on both sides of a remarkable bend in Saco River, extending in its circuit . . . more than thirty miles, and returning within seven miles of its former course.”

Freighter off Cape Elizabeth, from South Portland, Maine

Dwight described Portland, the goal of this journey, as being "built on a peninsula resembling the form of a saddle, the principal part of the houses being erected on the seat. The situation is handsome: the harbor, a beautiful piece of water spreading on the southeast, and the cove, smaller, but scarcely less beautiful, on the northwest. . . . The slope on which it is built furnishes everywhere a ready passage for all the water, and the happiest means of keeping the town perfectly clean. . . . The wells furnish an ample supply of pure and fine water. Accordingly, the inhabitants enjoy as uninterrupted health as those of any place of the same size in the United States."

Along the Eastern Promenade, Portland

Casco Bay, seen from the Eastern Promenade

Landscape at Chester, New Hampshire

The trip back from Portland was by way of Biddeford, through Wells and Berwick to Somersworth, New Hampshire, where they stayed at the inn that in their previous journey had led Dwight to contrast the sometimes ruffianly innkeepers of Great Britain with those in New England. (The latter by law had to be gentlemen of principle.) Several undulating farm communities followed. Of these, Dwight noted Chester in particular, not only as the most flourishing, but because it was the site of Rattlesnake Hill, an eminence reported to contain a cavern hung with stalactites "whose polished surfaces reflect the light of a torch with uncommon brilliancy."

Appleblossom time, Groton, Massachusetts, Mt. Wachusett beyond

Through Londonderry and across the Merrimack, a few miles above the great bend at Dracut, "under the auspices of a ferryman who seemed very much like a stranger to the world in which we lived," Dwight commented, they continued on to Groton. There they "found again the good land and the substantial farming character so remarkable in the county of Worcester." This town had had its share of terror under Indian attack 120 years before, when about forty of its "dwelling houses and the church, together with barns and outhouses" had been burned, shortly after the destruction of Lancaster, near by. The leader of the attack, John Monoco, was taken prisoner before he could execute his boastful threat to burn several more towns. He was "led through the streets of Boston with a halter about his neck, and hanged."

Left: *Pumunanquet, "he who shoots the stars," statue by Philip S. Sears, at Fruitlands in Harvard, Massachusetts*

Below: *Bronson Alcott's "New Eden" at Fruitlands, in the valley of the Nashua Indians, of whom Dwight writes*

The Bulfinch Church, Lancaster, built 1816, now a National Historic Landmark

Skirting the villages of Shirley and Harvard, the travelers went down the Nashua River valley to Lancaster, the site of what Dwight believed to be the first quarry of slate wrought in the United States. Lancaster settlers lived peacefully with their Indian neighbors, the Nashuas, under the leadership of Sholan, their sachem, and his successor. But in 1675 King Philip succeeded in drafting the Nashuas into his scheme of "extirpating the English," and several times in the next thirty-five years the town came near to destruction.

According to Dwight, because its surface was hilly and rough, Sterling "continued to be a forest until a late period. Like other modern settlements, it has had no share in Indian depredations. Sterling was the residence of Sholan, the upright sachem of the Nashuas." It became a township in 1781.

Street junction at Sterling, Massachusetts, site of famous "Baltimore Chair" manufacture

From "Princeton, another rich grazing township," Dwight reported, "the Blue Hills in Milton and the waters of Boston Harbor, distant fifty miles, can both be seen here in a clear day. . . ." They continued on their ways over leaf-strewn roads, to New Haven, with fall colors reminding them of springtime to come and the year's rounding out to the next journey of discovery.

Along a farm road, Princeton, Massachusetts

The leaf-covered green at Brimfield, Massachusetts

CONNECTICUT AND VERMONT

Cove, Long Island Sound, at Rowayton, Connecticut

Farm scene, Valley of the Black River, Vermont

Moss Glen Falls, Granville Gulf, Vermont, in the Green Mountains

The granite quarry at Barre, Vermont

A pastoral scene, western highlands near Brookfield, Connecticut

Journey to Vergennes

IN most of his journeys Dwight went up the Connecticut River Valley, but not this time, for on his way to Vergennes, he and his companion followed the Housatonic River and traveled a route almost exactly that of Number 7 on today's maps.

The settlement and the quality of the majority of villages in Connecticut were determined by its rivers and valleys rather than by its coastal shoreline. The inhabitants—most of whom had chosen to build in a place where "life may be passed through more pleasantly than in most others . . . not where trade compels, but where happiness invites to settle"—Dwight found far more healthful than those of the South. He calculates that the chance of living beyond the age of forty-five in New England as compared to Georgia, for example, was 2 to 1.

At the time he was writing, Connecticut contained about 5,000 square miles, with a population that had increased from 251,002 in 1800 by close to 11,000 in the next ten years. Of its government, Dwight says: "I suspect, there is not a state in the world where an individual is of more, perhaps of as much importance in the mere character of a man as in this community."

He believed that Vermont, through which they also traveled extensively, would become a manufacturing country: "This state is extremely well watered by small rivers, brooks, and springs. Almost every farm has its rivulet, and every town its millstream. . . . Wool, flax, hemp, and iron are the produce of its own grounds; the cotton its inhabitants can easily procure in any quantities. Streams and millseats fitted for every kind of machinery of which water is the moving principle abound everywhere, and the inhabitants are sufficiently ingenious to form and manage successfully every engine of this nature. . . .

"A considerable part of all those who *begin* the cultivation of the wilderness may be denominated *foresters or pioneers*," Dwight observes. They "cut down trees, build log houses, lay open forested grounds to cultivation, and prepare the way for those who come after them," before they move on restlessly to other wilderness. A better husbandman, seeing the advantages of broken ground and a dwelling, buys it from the first man, farms the land, and "changes the desert into a fruitful field."

Dwight believed that many of those who first claimed and acquired influence in Vermont "were men of loose principles and loose morals. . . ." But he prophesies that under the "influence of the New England institutions on the present and succeeding generations," Vermont would become an "important nursery of the human race . . . and a country where a great mass of happiness and virtue may be fairly expected in future ages." For, as they had in their journeys to Maine, Dwight and his companion met with exceptional individuals on this one—men who had not only opened up parcels of the land, but were staying upon them to produce the roots of the civilization that bears the peculiar and endearing stamp of New England.

Their journey through western Connecticut and Massachusetts and through the mountains of Vermont to Vergennes began on September 16, 1798.

Litchfield Hills landscape near Goshen, Connecticut

Without preamble, Dwight began the detailed observations of terrain, housing, industry, morals, and population that are so characteristic of his journeying. In the Litchfield area, the "open extensive valleys, hills gracefully arched, rich hollows, and groves formed of lofty trees interspersed everywhere at the most pleasing distances" were an ever renewed delight to his eyes. Goshen he found in many places "handsome, being formed of easy slopes and open valleys. It is perhaps the best grazing ground in the state; and the inhabitants are probably more wealthy than any other collection of farmers in New England equally numerous. The quantity of cheese made by them annually is estimated at four hundred thousand pounds weight." In 1800, their population was less than 1,500, so their wealth derived from a lot more than "the superiority of grazing ground to that which is devoted to tillage," to which Dwight ascribed it; they must have been an extremely industrious group as well.

The rapid Housatonic River, from the shore at West Cornwall, Connecticut

Stockbridge Mission House, built 1739

Following the Housatonic and skirting a spur of the Green Mountain Range, they reached Stockbridge and stopped at the Mission House erected there as a place where the Stockbridge Indians could be "Christianized" and where for seven years the great Jonathan Edwards, Timothy Dwight's grandfather, was the missionary in charge. It is interesting that the history of this tribe, which Timothy discussed, was to him an instance of "an Indian tradition directly asserting in terms which cannot easily be misconstrued that the Americans, partly at least, came from the eastern shore of Asia" by way of the Straits of Bering, finally reaching the borders of the Hudson River where "they settled and spread through the neighboring country."

The Housatonic River springs from three sources, according to Dwight. It is the western branch that passes through New Ashford, Pittsfield, and Lenox in a generally southerly direction. It then turns westward through Stockbridge and around Monument Mountain, the burial place of an Indian who had apparently disgraced his tribe, before it turns south again.

The Valley of the Housatonic at Stockbridge, Massachusetts

Passing through a land that went from lovely intervals along the river, and gentle farmlands sloping far distances below mountain spurs, to hills "of uncouth forms and sudden acclivities," such as those they found in New Ashford, they approached Williamstown, lying "principally in a triangular valley, bounded by Williamstown Mountain on the south, the range of the Green Mountains on the east, and that of Taconic on the west. These ranges approach near each other on the north, leaving a narrow opening into Pownal. . . . The scenery as a whole is pleasant, but more distinguished for sublimity than beauty."

Cattle grazing beneath Berkshire Hills, near Williamstown, Massachusetts

Morning fog from the Taconic Trail through the Taconic Mountains in Massachusetts

Dandelions in the Berkshire Hills, Massachusetts

The eastern part of Pownal, Dwight wrote, "lies on a rough, tedious hill, the surface unpleasant, the soil moist, but cold and unproductive; the houses also were ordinary, and the inhabitants apparently unthrifty." But it was here that he saw clouds that called upon all his eloquence of description. "All these the setting sun tinged throughout with a purple of the most exquisite hue. If the Tyrian dye was a fourth part as beautiful, I cannot wonder that it was coveted by emperors. . . ." And the camera's-eye view of the Hoosic Valley at Pownal (see over) certainly belies Dwight's rather jaundiced judgment of the area.

The Pownal Country Store, Pownal, Vermont

Panorama of the Hoosic Valley, taken at Pownal

Bennington Dwight found quite different, though it was but a few miles north of Pownal. Its soil, he reported, "is of the first quality, and equally suited to all the productions of the climate. Wheat and grass, the extremes of agricultural vegetation, grow here luxuriantly and alike. The pastures, even at this period of the year, were covered with rich and abundant herbage, and appeared in many places like meadows rather than like fields in which cattle had fed through the whole preceding season."

Pastoral scene at Bennington, Vermont

Bennington Monument silhouetted against a summer sky

A typical barn at Shaftsbury, Vermont

Manchester village street in the fall

The Morgan Horse Farm, University of Vermont, Middlebury

After being held up by a wild storm at Shaftsbury, of which Dwight's description reminds one of a turgid, light-streaked Hudson River School painting, the travelers skirted small towns (for each of which Dwight dutifully provided census figures for 1790, 1800, and 1810), stopping at Manchester, "built on a single street . . . lying along a beautiful plain for about a mile"; spending the night at Rutland; and then on to Middlebury, the latter part of their journey through a thick forest at night. "We trembled through this part of our way," Dwight wrote. He was extremely scornful of the mile-square city of Vergennes, which was set up by Colonel Ethan Allan, and named in honor of the French minister of Foreign Affairs, Count de Vergennes, "whom ardent, uninformed, and shortsighted Americans at that time believed to be a friend to this country." Allan had planned it to be the Vermont seat of government.

The main street, Vergennes

Driftwood fence near Bridport, Vermont

Farm scene at Shoreham, southwest of Vergennes

Champlain Valley, looking west

On this trip to Vergennes Dwight went over into New York after traveling east of Lake Champlain for some miles, through Bridport, Shoreham, Benson, and other towns to Fair Haven, with occasional glimpses of the lake shore and its wide margin of bulrushes. They returned to Richmond, Massachusetts, by way of New Lebanon, New York, and on down to Salisbury, past Mount Riga and Bald Peak Mountain, for one last look at the grandeur of the Taconic Range before re-entering the Housatonic Valley at Sharon. A tumultuous cataract, five miles below, was the climax of this part of their journey. They crossed what is now the Appalachian Trail near Kent and went on the rest of the way through Litchfield to New Haven without incident.

Sunset along the grassy shores of Lake Champlain

Wood road, Salisbury, Connecticut

MASSACHUSETTS AND RHODE ISLAND

A threatening sky over furrowed lands in the Berkshires

Wataquadock Hill on the Bay Path Indian Trail, Bolton

Opposite: *The Old Windmill at Eastham, Massachusetts*

Mt. Greylock, North Adams, Massachusetts, from the Hairpin Turn on the Mohawk Trail

Rockport, Massachusetts, Harbor, always busy with boats

Riding the surf at Newport, Rhode Island

The beach and lighthouse at Watch Hill, Westerly, Rhode Island

Interior of Gilbert Stuart's birthplace, Saunderstown, Rhode Island

Journey to Provincetown

THE history of the coastland areas of Connecticut, Rhode Island, and Massachusetts through which this journey carried Dwight and two companions is studded with references to Indians, both friendly and hostile.

Here Sassacus, principal sachem of the Pequots when the first colonists arrived, early foresaw the destruction of his people and tried unsuccessfully to unite them against the intruders, in what has been called the Pequot War. He was apparently an extraordinary man, who, Dwight notes, "appears to have been regarded by his neighbors, as well as by his subjects, with that peculiar awe which is inspired by superior personal strength, activity, courage, and cunning."

The sachem Momanguin, in Connecticut, and Massassoit, in Massachusetts, saw the colonists as protection against Sassacus and sold them land. The Narragansets of Rhode Island outnumbered the Pequots, but hated Sassacus so that they made a treaty with the British, whom they hated only a little less.

From 1634 on, the Pequots besieged and murdered where they could, particularly in the Saybrook area, despite an agreement they had made to "yield their right to Connecticut River and its neighborhood to the English." In 1636 a small band of English under Captain John Mason, assisted by friendly but fearful Indians, destroyed the Pequot fortress on the Mystic River. The people of Sassacus were so angered by the defeat that they finally turned against him. They disbanded after destroying their own wigwams and his remaining fortress near the Thames River. With some of his chiefs and followers, he joined the Iroquois, but most of his tribe fled to the west of the Connecticut, where they were pursued and conquered by the colonists.

New England then had respite from general Indian warfare until Philip, the son of Massassoit, took up again the plan to unite all Indians against the English in a futile war which lasted from June 1675 to his death in August 1676, during which the Narragansets were also vanquished. By the time Dwight arrived upon the scene, Indians were living on land granted by the legislature. They worked within the white man's system, and they had lost all ambition.

Dwight acknowledges this with a combination of understanding and rather stiff-necked righteousness shortly after he and two alumni of Yale began to journey toward Cape Cod through the villages that lay on the shores of Long Island Sound. The only way the Indian could be saved, he concludes, would be through conversion to Christianity, or establishment in him of the love of property, the substitute in every civilized nation, according to Dwight, for the Indian love of glory.

The Journey to Provincetown began on September 17, 1800, the first of many travels that Dwight was to make through New England early in the nineteenth century.

The journey began with a thirty-four-mile ride to Saybrook, passing through East Haven with its fine oyster beds near the mouth of the Quinnipiac River; Branford "destitute of beauty"; and Guilford with its old stone houses, particularly that of the Reverend Henry Whitfield. All these coastal towns, Dwight found, relied upon whitefish for manure (10,000 were considered a rich dressing for one acre). They were seined in tremendous quantities ("A single net," Dwight reported, "has taken two hundred thousand in a day . . . sold for a dollar a thousand. . . ").

The Whitfield House, Guilford, Connecticut

The shore at Fenwick Point, Old Saybrook, Connecticut

Saybrook had its origin in 1635 in a hastily set up fort on Fenwick Point, "on a rising ground of considerable height jutting into the river, and united to the main by a beach and salt marsh which borders it on both sides." Two cannon mounted here effectively kept Dutch intruders out. Later a permanent fortification was put up and was a protection against enemies on land as well as from the sea.

Country lane in the early spring, Old Saybrook

The inhabitants of Saybrook, Dwight found, "retain most of their original character, and are proverbially distinguished in the country around them for their peace and good neighborhood. Decency, good order, and quiet have with little interruption prevailed from the original settlement. At the same time, they exhibit proofs of moderate industry and contentment rather than of vigorous enterprise. This part of Saybrook has, I suspect, increased very little within the last thirty or forty years. The additional numbers become colonists and emigrate to the north and the west."

From Saybrook the travelers crossed the Connecticut to Lyme, then on to New London. According to legend, these towns had claimed title to the same piece of land when the seat of government was a hazardous fifty miles away. They decided to settle the matter themselves. Each town chose two boxers: "On a day mutually appointed, the champions appeared in the field, and fought with their fists, till victory declared in favor of each of the Lyme combatants. . . . This," Dwight remarked, "it is presumed, is the only instance in which a public controversy has been decided in New England by pugilism."

Mouth of the Connecticut River at Old Lyme

Interior, the Thomas Lee House, East Lyme, built 1660

New London, which later developed whaling as an industry, was described by Dwight as having a harbor where "vessels of almost any size find in it sufficient water and good anchoring ground. It is also perfectly safe." In 1781 the town was taken by the British under particularly brutal circumstances as related by Dwight, and set afire under the orders of Benedict Arnold. Part of Groton, opposite New London, which had originally been the principal seat of the Pequot Indians, also went up in flames under Arnold's orders.

The Old Town Mill, New London, established 1650

119 "Whale Oil Row," New London

The Charles W. Morgan, *at Mystic, Connecticut, with prow of the* Joseph Conrad, *foreground*

At Stonington Dwight found much to his liking. The soil was rich and yielded maize, oats, barley and rye. The farms contained sixty to three hundred acres each and were cultivated by tenants—mostly from the poorer state of Rhode Island—a circumstance which Dwight remarked upon because he had not found it in practice to such a degree anywhere else.

Door front, Old Stonington, Connecticut, Lighthouse (1823)

Newport, Rhode Island, street scene

"Newport is acknowledged to be the best fish market in the United States," Dwight reported, and listed 112 different varieties of fish caught in neighboring waters. The town "was settled in 1639 by Mr. William Coddington and seventeen others," who "favored the peculiar tenets of Mrs. Hutchinson. . . . In the year 1637, he and his companions purchased this island. . . . Here he soon after settled himself with several of his associates. Mr. Hutchinson speedily followed him with his family; and, by the zeal and activity of his wife, was chosen governor in the place of Mr. Coddington, whom this restless, turbulent woman, incapable of any enjoyment unless when controlling both the civil and ecclesiastical affairs of the community in which she lived, persuaded the inhabitants to lay aside."

Left: *Square rigger anchored at Newport*
Below: *The waterfront at Newport*

Old Colony House (1739), Washington Square, Newport

The harbor of Newport, recognized by President Adams as an excellent naval base and fortified under his auspices, was at one time desired by the French, who unsuccessfully urged Congress to cede it to them, so that they could "protect" the coast. Dwight found the town still suffering from effects of the Revolution. "The commerce of Newport was formerly extensive, but was destroyed in the Revolutionary War. A part of the inhabitants were driven off, and the part which remained behind were not a little distressed by their invaders."

Houses built in the 1800's still survive along Cliff Walk in all their ornate glory. During Dwight's time, the well-bred people of Newport, he observed, had "the same polished, agreeable manners which prevail along the eastern coast of Massachusetts. The decay of business has produced here its customary consequences. The men of wealth live by loaning their money without entering in any great degree into active, useful business. The poor people catch fish for their sustenance, and lounge and saunter for their pleasure."

Along the Cliff Walk, Newport

Narragansett Bay from West Main Road, Portsmouth, Rhode Island

New Bedford was a prosperous whaling town in Dwight's day. "Fifteen thousand tons of shipping belong to this port," he wrote, "the great body of which is owned by the inhabitants. It is chiefly made up of large vessels employed in the whale fishery about Falkland Islands, in the Pacific Ocean, and elsewhere, or in a circuitous carrying trade." Today, New Bedford's busy seafront still bears marks of that era.

Left: *Whaleman Statue, by Bella Pratt, at New Bedford, Massachusetts*

Below: *Figurehead sign at New Bedford*

Cape Cod Canal, looking southeast

Crossing the isthmus which connected the peninsula of Cape Cod with the main between Wareham and Sandwich, "the horse may be said to wade," Dwight remarked. At this time the Cape Cod Canal had long been a project under discussion. "The importance of this work . . . is so great that it will probably be one day attempted," Dwight reported. "During five months out of the nine in which it would be open, easterly storms more or less prevail. Many vessels are lost, and a great mass of property is sunk in the ocean. The commerce of Boston and other towns on the eastern shore of Massachusetts would also be rendered so much safer and easier that it could not fail of being greatly increased. Perhaps there never was a spot in which such a work was more necessary, or in which it would be more useful to mankind, than in this. The distance between the navigable waters of these two bays is five miles."

Footbridge across the marshes, Sandwich, Massachusetts

The Hoxie House, Sandwich, supposedly oldest Cape style house

The town of Sandwich "is built on the northern, or as it is commonly called, the western side of the isthmus, on a hill of considerable height. The most compact part of it surrounds a clear, pleasant looking pond," wrote Dwight. "From this . . . runs a handsome stream, on which stands a gristmill. The church is an ancient building, as are also many of the houses. A considerable salt marsh along the shore of the bay yields the inhabitants a large quantity of hay, which is valuable both as fodder and as manure. Near it is a small harbor, called the Town Harbor, where, and in some other inlets belonging to the township, about thirty vessels are employed in the coasting business, especially in carrying wood to Boston."

"The houses in Yarmouth," Dwight reported, "are inferior to those in Barnstable, and much more generally of the class which may be called with propriety Cape Cod houses. These have one story and four rooms on the lower floor, and are covered on the sides, as well as the roofs, with pine shingles, eighteen inches in length. The chimney is in the middle immediately behind the front door, and on each side of the door are two windows. The roof is straight. Under it are two chambers, and there are two larger and two smaller windows in the gable end. This is the general structure and appearance of the great body of houses from Yarmouth to Race Point. . . . The barns are usually neat, but always small."

The Colonel John Thacher House (1680) at Yarmouth, Massachusetts

Typical Cape Cod landscape at Barnstable

On their way to Orleans, they stood upon a high ground in Barnstable, and Dwight described the scene: "A very extensive salt marsh, at that time covered with several thousand stacks of hay; the harbor, a mile wide, and four or five miles long; a long, lofty, wild and fantastical beach, thrown into a thousand grotesque forms by the united force of winds and waves; and the bay, bounded on the north only by sky, on the east by the peninsula of Cape Cod, and on the west by the eastern shore of Massachusetts. . . ."

Nauset Beach and grasses along the shore at Eastham, Massachusetts

"In Eastham," Dwight wrote, "the surface became a perfect plain, and the peninsula so narrow that we had a full view of Massachusetts Bay and the Atlantic at the same time.... On the driest and most barren of grounds grows a plant which I had never seen, known here by the name of beach grass." This grass which inhabitants were required by law to plant every April, as in other towns in New England they had to repair highways, was "set out in the sand at distances of three feet. After one row was set, others were placed behind it in such a manner as to shut up the interstices; or, as a carpenter would say, *so as to break the joints* . . . in order to prevent the wind from having an open course through the grass in any direction, lest it should drive the sand away.... But for this single, unsightly vegetable, the slender barrier which here has so long resisted the ravages of the ocean had not improbably been long since washed away. In the ruins, Provincetown and its most useful harbor must have been lost; and the relief which the harbor and the inhabitants furnish to multitudes of vessels in distress, and which no other place or people could possibly furnish, must have been prevented."

Opposite: *Dunes at Highland Light, Truro*

Provincetown Harbor taken from the Town Wharf

"The fishery of Provincetown," wrote Dwight, "is an important object." Whales, after being scarce for some years, were coming back. "The cod fishery is pursued with great spirit and success. Just before we arrived, a schooner came in from the Great Banks with 56,000 fish, about 1,500 quintals, taken in a single voyage: the main deck, as I was informed, being on her return eight inches under water in calm weather. . . .

"The harbor . . . is sufficient for ships of any size, and it will contain more than three thousand vessels at once. . . There is no other harbor on a windward shore within two hundred miles. A vast number of vessels are always plying in this commercial region, and thousands have found safety here which would otherwise have perished."

"A stranger born and educated in the interior of New England," Dwight commented, "amid the varied beauties of its surface and the luxuriant succession of its produce, naturally concludes when he visits Provincetown that the inhabitants . . . must possess a very limited share of enjoyment. Facts, however, refute this conclusion. . . . Food and clothing, houses, lodging, and fuel, they possess of such a quality and with so much ease in the acquisition as to satisfy all the demands of that middle state in life which wise men of every age have dignified by the name of *golden*. Nature and habit endear them to the place in which they were born and live, and prevent them from feeling what would be serious inconveniences to a stranger. Their mode of life is naturally not less pleasing than that of the farmer or mechanic, for no

Fishing boats anchored at a Provincetown wharf

people are more attached to their employment than seamen. . . . The draft of herrings, the fare of codfish, the conquest of a shark, and the capture of a whale prompt their ambition, engross their care, and furnish pleasures as entirely unknown to the farmer as the joy of harvest is to them. . . . Almost every day strangers visit Provincetown from different parts of the world: for there is hardly any spot, except great trading cities, which is more frequented by vessels of all descriptions than this. . . . While the husbandman has followed the plow or brandished the sickle, the inhabitant of Provincetown has coasted the shores of Greenland, swept the Brazilian seas, or crossed the Pacific Ocean in chase of the whale. . . ."

Provincetown waterfront

They went back by way of Plymouth, "the first town built in New England by civilized men . . . inferior in worth," Dwight noted, "to no body of men whose names are recorded in history during the last seventeen hundred years. A kind of venerableness arising from these facts attaches to this town, which may be termed a prejudice. Still it has its foundation in the nature of man, and will never be eradicated either by philosophy or ridicule. No New Englander who is willing to indulge his native feelings can stand upon the rock where our ancestors set the first foot after their arrival on the American shore without experiencing emotions entirely different from those which are excited by any common object of the same nature. . . ."

Plymouth Bay, haven of the Pilgrims

Statue of Massasoit, friend of the Pilgrims, in Plymouth, Massachusetts

Left: *Typical Pilgrim house interior at Plimoth Plantation*

Below: *Plimoth Plantation, replica of the original Pilgrim colony of 1627*

Burial Hill at Plymouth, overlooking the harbor

Standing upon Burial Hill, Dwight paid tribute to the Plymouth colonists: "The institutions, civil, literary, and religious, by which New England is distinguished on this side of the Atlantic began here. Here the manner of holding lands in free socage, now universal in this country, commenced. Here the right of suffrage was imparted to every citizen. . . . Here was formed the first . . . local legislature which is called a town meeting, and . . . the first parochial school was set up. . . . Here also the first building was erected for the worship of God, the first religious assembly gathered, and the first minister called and settled by the voice of the church and congregation. On these simple foundations has since been erected a structure of good order, peace, liberty, knowledge, morals, and religion, to which nothing on this side of the Atlantic can bear a remote comparison."

Volume II

CONNECTICUT AND MASSACHUSETTS

Congregational Church Steeple, Greenfield Hill, Connecticut

The Connecticut River at Middletown, Connecticut

Opposite: *Village church, Cornwall Bridge, Connecticut*

Houses on the village green at Guilford, Connecticut, winter

Goodspeed's Opera House, East Haddam, Connecticut

A tobacco farm at Windsor, Connecticut

First Church of Christ, Longmeadow, Massachusetts

Pioneer Valley at Hadley, Massachusetts

Curving furrows, Amherst, Massachusetts

Connecticut River from Valley Sugar Loaf Mountain, in Massachusetts

Street scene, Old Deerfield, Massachusetts

Journey to Canada

EACH of the major journeys Timothy Dwight and his companions took began near the mouth of the noble Connecticut. He recorded thirteen of these, and nearly half included many miles along this stream, which, he writes, "may perhaps with as much propriety as any in the world be named the 'beautiful river'."

By the time he started out on this first major journey after the turn of the nineteenth century, Dwight had reason to feel that he was well qualified to discuss the length and breadth of the Connecticut, its intervals, its valleys, and the people who lived upon its borders and were sustained for the most part by its beneficence. For he had already made three trips up and down most of its length. He never ceased to marvel at the industry of the colonists who struck inward from the security of the waterways and substituted settlements for forests. In Maine, New Hampshire, Vermont, Massachusetts, and New York he passed the dwellings of several hundred thousand "of these people, erected on grounds that in 1760 were an absolute wilderness."

The Connecticut, the Merrimack, the Saco, the Piscataqua, the Kennebec, the Penobscot—to mention only some of the great streams of New England—were all avenues of exploration as well as settlement. Villages grew up near the mouths of these rivers and along the coast where the sea itself was the major roadway. Gradually settlement worked inward. Water, not only for human sustenance, but for intercourse and industry, governed the existence of the explorers and first settlers of Connecticut, Massachusetts, and Rhode Island. Until searching eyes could discern from the air good landing areas anywhere in an unexplored interior, men used the rivers, anchoring their craft alongshore and cautiously hacking their way into the wilderness in search of more farmland.

In his *Travels* Dwight tends to dwell upon each state in general as he is about "to take his leave of it." He does the same for the Connecticut River during this trip, devoting three letters to a description of its lakes and tributary streams, its navigability, and the falls and shoals that interrupted it.

In one letter he discusses the Connecticut Valley, its "intervals" of fertile ground lying between the original bank of the river and the river itself, and its major expansions. In another, he discusses the people and the towns in the valley: "not, like those along the Hudson, mere collections of houses and stores clustered round a landing, where nothing but mercantile and mechanical business is done; where the inhabitants appear to form no connections or habits besides those which naturally grow out of bargains and sales; where the position of the store determines that of the house, and that of the wharf often commands both; where beauty of situation is disregarded and every convenience except that of trade is forgotten. On the contrary . . . the intention of settling them is not merely to acquire property, but to sustain the relations, perform the duties, and contribute to the enjoyments of life."

The twelve letters that cover the journey to the Canada line supply Dwight's characteristically encyclopedic data on the population, buildings, and industry of the towns he studied along the way, but they also delve into statistics of interest primarily to a farmer.

The lessons he had learned while farming the estates inherited from his father are reflected in his comments on the crops. He notes the growth of various species of corn in different areas of New England, he describes in detail the disadvantages of deep vegetable mold in the cultivation of apple trees, and describes how too much animal manure used in growing wheat can cause its blasting. His years as a farmer had given him practical proof of the balances maintained in nature and of the virtue of conservation.

Writing about the people of Newbury, Vermont, he observes that they appeared "to have cut down their forest with an improvident hand: an evil but too common in most parts of this country. Unhappily it is an increasing evil, and may hereafter put a final stop to the progress of population long before it will have reached to the natural acme. Almost every person complains of this imprudence; and yet not a single efficacious nor hopeful measure is adopted to lessen or even to check it. A farmer when employed in cutting down a grove rarely remembers that it will require thirty years to furnish on the same spot wood fit for fuel, and sixty to yield that which will become useful timber. As rarely does he recollect that the boughs and branches which he leaves to perish on the ground would supply warmth to one or two indigent families. Forecast is certainly no predominant trait in the character of man, else an evil of this magnitude would create very serious apprehensions."

Finally, Dwight speaks of the river itself: "The purity, salubrity, and sweetness of its waters; the frequency and elegance of its meanders; its absolute freedom from all aquatic vegetables; the uncommon and universal beauty of its banks, here a smooth and winding beach, there covered with rich verdure, now fringed with bushes, now crowned with lofty trees, and now formed by the intruding hill, the rude bluff, the shaggy mountain, are objects which no traveler can thoroughly describe, and no reader adequately imagine. When to these are added the numerous towns, villages, and hamlets almost everywhere exhibiting the mark of prosperity and improvement, the rare appearance of decline, the numerous churches lifting their spires in frequent succession, the neat schoolhouses everywhere occupied, and the mills busied on such a multitude of streams, it may safely be asserted that a pleasanter journey will rarely be found than that which is made in the Connecticut Valley."

It was upon such a journey that on Tuesday, September 20, 1803, Timothy Dwight and four unnamed companions set out to go upriver to the line that divides New England from Lower Canada.

Rooftops of New Haven

The first day Timothy Dwight's party rode thirty-four miles, from New Haven to Hartford. "Had a less rigid attention been given to the scheme of making a straight road," Dwight noted, a bit acidly, concerning the road completed between the two towns since his 1797 journey, "several disagreeable hills might have been avoided, much of the expense prevented, and the distance very little increased." But he had to admit that nevertheless it was one of the better roads in the state, and it did shorten the distance between New Haven and Hartford by about five miles.

Quinnipiac Valley at Meriden, Connecticut, from Castle Craig

About three miles before they reached the Quinnipiac River, which "runs through a large expansion of meadows with a succession of meanders, peculiarly elegant," Dwight wrote, they stopped to visit the "manufactory of firearms" erected by Eli Whitney, inventor of the cotton gin that increased—literally by one thousand—a person's ability to separate cotton fibers from the seed. Dwight digressed at some length upon the story of this genius whose invention brought so much wealth to the South and so little to himself—and that after thirteen years of lawsuits.

Orchard stand, Meriden

Trees in Old Deerfield, Massachusetts

Dwight merely mentioned some of the towns on the way to Brattleboro, their next destination—New Britain, Newington, Northampton, Hatfield, Whately, Deerfield, Greenfield, Bernardston, Guilford. Near the last, the first township in Vermont on their road, was the site of Fort Dummer, erected under the supervision of one of Dwight's ancestors.

From the valley of the Quinnipiac, and along the road where the river wound "in a sprightly manner," then crossing Newington Mountain ridge, skirting or riding through familiar towns, the travelers feasted their eyes on the "rich prospect of the Connecticut Valley with all its interesting appendages."

Greenfield, Massachusetts, snow scene, taken from above the town

In all his travels, Dwight never ceased to appreciate the verdure, the produce, along the great Connecticut, and the contrasts between the quiet village greens in its valley and the "shaggy eminences" that in some places shut out both morning and evening sun.

Brattleboro was the second spot in Vermont settled by English inhabitants, according to Dwight. "A little collection of houses, often styled the Village, and sometimes the City, built at the southern limit of a plain immediately below the mouth of West River, is one of the prettiest objects of the kind and size within my recollection. If we did not mistake in counting them, they were now but ten in number, but with their appendages were remarkably neat. . . ." Above Brattleboro, between Westminster and Lyme, Dwight revisited Bellows Falls. In 1797, a canal for the purpose of conveying boats around the falls was about two-thirds finished. By 1803 it was functioning beautifully. The first bridge over the Connecticut had been built in 1785 by Colonel Enoch Hale, just below the principal fall. He had the imagination and courage to override the ridicule and objections of townspeople who saw the whole project as romantic and impractical. Though that bridge had been taken down and a new one built by 1803, Hale had shown the way, and thirteen bridges were slung across the Connecticut by 1797.

Bridge at Bellows Falls, Vermont

House at Westminster, Vermont

Lyme, New Hampshire, Congregational Church doorway, built in 1812

Meandering by way of Dummerston, Putney, Westminster, and Rockingham on the Vermont side of the Connecticut, Dwight and his party arrived at Charlestown, on the New Hampshire side, where they spent the weekend. To Windsor next, and continuing along the New Hampshire side through Hanover, Lyme, Orford, and Piermont, they rode to Haverhill, "a well-appearing town," on "a handsome elevation overlooking the adjacent country many miles north and south, and not less than six or seven from east to west." About five miles north of Haverhill, when traveling the same route in 1797, Dwight had found debris and disorder, corduroy roads, fallen or girdled trees that had not yet died and fallen as the result of the girdling, stumps, and crude log houses. Now these were replaced by "good farmers' houses, and not infrequently those which were handsome. . . . The number of mills had also been considerably increased; and one of them . . . yielded the proprietor $1,000 a year. The quantity of boards and scantling lying by the side of it certainly gave some color to the story. . . . Over all was diffused an undisturbed serenity."

Haverhill, New Hampshire

They traveled along the Lower Ammonoosuc toward Rosebrook's Inn, where Dwight had enjoyed staying in 1797. The river, Dwight noted, "rises in the White Mountains and runs a course of fifty miles. Its waters are everywhere pure; its bed clean, being composed of rocks, stones, or gravel; and its current gentle and rapid by turns, but always sprightly. . . ." The river road "runs at the foot of the hills on the northern side, whose cliffs and woods, overhanging the stream, form with their wild magnificence a fine contrast to the softer scenery by which they are succeeded. From this spot, the river, during a progress of fifteen miles, winds with an elegant course through a chain of intervals parted into rich farms. . . .

"Seven miles from our inn . . . we crossed the river by a very difficult ford, just below a place called Upper Mills. Here we left the valley, and ascended the high hills of Bethlehem. The road through this township lies partly in a forest and partly amid the settlements. These are recent, few, poor, and planted on a soil singularly rough and rocky. There is nothing in Bethlehem which merits notice except the patience, enterprise, and hardihood of the settlers which have induced them to venture and stay upon so forbidding a spot, a magnificent prospect of the White Mountains, and a splendid collection of other mountains in their neighborhood, particularly on the southwest."

Scene along the Connecticut River in the town of Wells River, Vermont

Covered bridge and waterfall, Ammonoosuc River at Bath, New Hampshire

The Lower Ammonoosuc River, north of Bath

Franconia Notch area in New Hampshire

Franconia Range

"It is hardly necessary to observe," commented Dwight, "that the beauty of every fine landscape arises in a great measure from a comparison of the several objects which compose it, and is made up extensively of the relations which they bear to each other. This is emphatically true of a cluster of mountains. A nobler group cannot be imagined than that which is seen from Bethlehem, nor one to which this remark can be applied with more force. Their form, their extent, their height, their position, and all the circumstances of their appearance are so varied through the several gradations of beauty, boldness, and grandeur, and so happily related to each other that the eye finds here everything which can gratify its wishes in rude, wild, and magnificent scenery."

From Franconia Notch, Dwight and his companions visited the Flume. "The splendor of the cascade was greatly enhanced by every ascent; and the whole prospect, changing from beauty to sublimity, left the mind in a mixture of astonishment and rapture."

Echo Lake, Franconia Notch

Snow-clad Presidential Range at Jefferson, New Hampshire

"We had now reached the utmost limit of our intended excursion to these mountains," wrote Dwight. "Bidding adieu therefore to this singular combination of wild and awful magnificence," they left the Notch, and having taken dinner at Rosebrook's, continued to Jefferson, which lies in the bottom of a vast basin "watered through its whole length by Israel River. The mountains of Littleton protrude their bold and lofty promontories into its southwestern border, and the White Mountains bound it upon the southeast with a grandeur indescribable."

Valley and hills at Lancaster, New Hampshire

"Handsomer and richer lands probably do not exist. The hills which limit this valley on the west by their happily varied forms and moderate heights furnish one interesting variety in the picture. The valley of the Ammonoosuc is scooped with uncommon beauty, the surface bending with a graceful, inverted arch from the river to the summit of the mountains by which it is bounded on the north."

Covered bridge across the Upper Ammonoosuc at Groveton, New Hampshire

Mt. Monadnock, Lemington, Vermont

Farm at Colebrook, New Hampshire

Back and forth between New Hampshire and Vermont the travelers continued their way along the river. No doubt they feasted their eyes upon the early October foliage, though Dwight, intent upon facts of geography and agriculture, did not allude to it. Everything in Colebrook exhibited the "activity and enterprise of its inhabitants," he commented, "their roads, plantations, barns, and schoolhouses. Their barns are large and good, and their schoolhouses well built." About two miles below the inn where they lodged stood the "lofty mountain called the Grand Monadnock, in Lymington in Vermont, ascending immediately from the river, and rising above its level about two thousand feet."

Passing through a part of Canaan, Vermont, on October 4, the travelers crossed the Connecticut at a ford in Stewart, where the river was about fifty yards wide, and rode two miles more to the Canada line, their final destination. They were told that New Englanders had settled well beyond the border. "A person who has extensively seen the efforts of the New England people colonizing new countries," Dwight commented, "cannot fail of being forcibly struck by their enterprise, industry, and perseverance. . . . There are minds to whom little else than romantic adventures, splendid villas and palaces, the pomp of courts, the progress of armies, the glory of victories, and other magnificent displays of wealth and power can give even a transient pleasure. To me there is something far more delightful in contemplating the diffusion of enterprise and industry over an immense forest, where no oppression gives birth to the efforts of man, no sufferings have preceded the splendor, and no sacrifice of life, or even of comfort, is necessary to the existence of the triumph. The process is here all voluntary and free."

Street corner, Canaan, Vermont

Street scene, Stewartstown, New Hampshire

Having reached their goal, the Canadian border, the travelers turned around, and returned to Colebrook, where they stayed through a "copious rainfall," which gave Dwight the opportunity to provide the reader with a dissertation on vegetation, fish, animals, birds, and weather indigenous to the area.

The following day they traveled thirty-six miles back to Lancaster, and spent the night; then they proceeded to Bath, Dalton, Littleton, and Concord. The following morning, they went through Bradford to Newbury, Vermont, and across the Connecticut to Orford in a ferryboat managed by two astonishingly small children. "Immediately below the ferry," Dwight wrote, "lies a remarkable interval, extensively known in New England by the name of the *Great Oxbow*, and still more extensively by the name of the *Lower Coos*. This is a peninsula containing about nine hundred acres and washed on three sides by the river winding in the form of a beautiful bow. The isthmus which connects it with Newbury is about half a mile in breadth, and the circuit of the bow about four miles. The whole extent is one vast meadow, covered with the richest verdure, except a small tract converted into arable ground; and it is scarcely possible for mere earth to exhibit a more beautiful surface."

Overleaf: *The oxbow of the Connecticut River at Newbury, Vermont*

The main street of Orford, New Hampshire

Dartmouth College, Hanover, New Hampshire

Old fort at Charlestown, New Hampshire

After a night at Orford, they rode to Dartmouth, for the weekend, then on to Charlestown and its two hundred-year-old fort. In an earlier trip, Dwight had described in detail a siege by a large contingent of French Canadians and Indians in 1747, during which the Americans held their ground without losing a single man, in spite of repeated enemy attempts to burn the fort down.

Dartmouth College, founded in 1769 by the Rev. Eleazer Wheelock, was "intended especially for the education of Indians and of missionaries to the Indians."

The man most responsible for the funds used in building it was himself an Indian ordained as a minister after being educated at Wheelock's first academy, in Lebanon, Connecticut. Samson Occom was sent to England, where he preached so eloquently that funds for the new college poured in, but it did not become an institution for educating the Indians. Though, Dwight pointed out, the very ends at which the benefactors "perhaps especially aimed" were foiled, the seminary did provide a service "of extensive benefit to mankind."

Proceeding to Keene through Walpole and a corner of Surrey, the travelers were granted a "noble prospect. Immediately beneath the eye lies the Connecticut Valley on the west, and that of the Ashuelot on the east. The latter is about nine miles in length, and magnificently bounded by the range of Mount Washington, a long succession of lofty and varied eminences; far above all . . . ascends the conical summit of Monadnock. . . . A finer object can scarcely be conceived, nor a position in which it could be more advantageously seen."

Town of Keene, New Hampshire

Mt. Monadnock at Keene

"Keene is very pleasantly situated on the tongue of land between the two principal branches of the Ashuelot. The valley in which it is built extends, as we were informed, from north to south about forty miles in length. To the eye, in these directions, it is unlimited. The lands in this township are divided into hills, plains, and intervals, and are rich in all these varieties, yielding grass, flax, and every species of grain in abundance. . . . The intervals on both branches of the Ashuelot are extensive, and undoubtedly allured the first settlers hither at an early and dangerous period." From 1738, when it was settled, until the Peace of Paris in 1763, "the inhabitants had their full share of Indian incursions."

Along with those of Keene, the inhabitants of Swanzey deserted the area in 1745 after an Indian attack. But they went back and had rebuilt their houses along the beautiful, wide, peaceful Ashuelot ten years later, determined to stay. The Indians attacked again. "Their number was great, and the onset violent. But Captain Symes, their commander, defended it with such gallantry and perseverance that, after burning several buildings, killing the cattle, and destroying other property of the inhabitants, they withdrew. This was in June. In July, they invaded the town again, but with little success; and this seems to have been the last incursion made upon the Ashuelot."

The Ashuelot River at Swanzey, New Hampshire

An involved journey through Winchester, New Hampshire, across Millers River, Massachusetts, to Millers Falls, where they inspected a dam and canal, and through Montague, brought them to Sunderland, "a township formed of a tract on Mount Toby, a plain at its foot, and a considerable interval commencing within the town plat and extending several miles to the south.... Its inhabitants are sober, orderly, moral, economical, and moderately industrious. It is improving in its appearance, but leaves on the mind of a traveler a strong sense of still and sequestered life."

View of Sunderland, Massachusetts, from Sugar Loaf Mountain

Connecticut Valley farm at Amherst, Massachusetts

Dwight and his party had a particular reason for returning by way of Shutesbury rather than keeping close to the river. They went to see Ephraim Pratt, a man who was nearly 117 years old, and was said to have more than 1,500 descendants. He had been ill but once in his life, and looked not much above seventy, but Dwight wrote sadly, in concluding his account of the interview, "It is scarcely necessary to observe that a man 116 years old without religion was a melancholy sight to me."

They rode on to Amherst, of which Dwight wrote: "a handsomer piece of ground composed of hills and valleys is rarely seen; more elegant slopes, never" and thence, by quick stages, they traveled to New Haven.

VERMONT

The covered bridge between Windsor, Vermont, and Cornish, New Hampshire, longest covered-bridge span in the United States, first built in 1796

Covered bridge at Randolph, Vermont

Vermont landscape at East Montpelier, Vermont

Green Mountain hilltop view, Weston, Vermont

Skyscape, Grand Isle (South Hero), Vermont

Round barn at Albany, Vermont

Champlain Valley looking west, Burlington, Vermont

Cloudscape at Charlotte, Vermont

Lake Willoughby, Vermont

Journey to Western Vermont

DWIGHT really made the greater part of this journey three times. First, in 1798, he traveled to Vergennes. Then in 1806 he repeated the entire voyage, observing the changes eight years had wrought, and adding Burlington, St. Albans, Middlesex, Montpelier, and Randolph to the itinerary. In 1810, he took the same route again and interpolated notes from that trip into the text describing the previous journey.

As in the first trip, Dwight started up the Connecticut, then veered west for the second time, skirting the Green Mountains and making occasional excursions into New York across the western border of Vermont. Lake Champlain and its magnificent valley, lying between the Adirondack Mountains and the Green Mountains, with a Vermont shoreline of around one hundred and fifty miles, were the climax of the journey.

Dwight points out that the settlers who traveled westward from the coast and chose Vermont lands were for the most part restless "loners" who sought new challenges or the security of mountain heights where they could build fortresslike homes. Rough some of them were, unable to settle down into peaceful, law-abiding existence with other men. In fact, he viewed them with a somewhat jaundiced eye in 1798, for many of them were irreligious, thus, in his view, unprincipled, as well as too proud to bend to the needs of social intercourse. But it could have been that very pride that enabled them to turn rocky Vermont hills into dairy farmlands.

To them independence was worth every peril, even loss of life. It was worth the long period of lonely discomfort they had to face before they could have houses that were safe and gardens that would secure them the foods beyond those acquired with a fishing pole, a net, or a gun.

The summits of the hills in northwestern Vermont were fertile, though Dwight notes in writing about the succession of hills and valleys between Vergennes and Burlington: "What is uncommon where such a surface exists in New England, brooks and springs appeared to be rare." He was intrigued at Burlington by an unexplained phenomenon. Frogs, logs, and stumps were found at depths to forty feet, and in one case a boat at twelve feet, "within fifteen rods of Onion [Winooski] River." If the burials were caused by an earthquake or landslide, it could not have involved enough human life to make a mark on Dwight's time.

Of course, he also notes the fact that Vermont lumber was rafted from Burlington via Lake Champlain to Quebec; that quarrying marble was an important and growing industry of the state; that farm animals, hay and forage, and grasses for grazing covered Vermont hills.

The most pleasing aspect to Dwight in these journeys of 1806 and especially 1810, was that during the lapse between his first visit and these two later ones, a religious spirit had grown in several towns, including Benson, where he realizes vividly "what it is for the wilderness and solitary place to be glad, and the desert to rejoice and blossom as the rose."

With two companions, Dwight left New Haven on the trip that was to grant him this happy discovery, on Tuesday, September 16, 1806.

Berkshire Hills in winter at Williamstown, Massachusetts

Berkshire Hills in summer at Williamstown

Champlain Valley landscape, Charlotte, Vermont

In 1806, Dwight and his companions began traveling through the western part of Connecticut and Massachusetts, arriving at Williamstown three days later. He described this town as lying "principally in a triangular valley, bounded by Williamstown Mountain on the south, the range of the Green Mountains on the east, and that of Taconic on the west." He was intrigued by the free school there which became Williams College, named for Colonel Ephraim Williams, in whose will careful provisions had been made for its establishment.

Traveling into New York State briefly, and back into Vermont at Fairhaven, they went up through Middlebury, where Dwight's companions left him to visit Crown Point. He went on with new, casually found companions, to Vergennes, where his friends had already arrived. United again, they went to Burlington through Ferrisburg, Charlotte, and Shelburne. He found Charlotte "a beautiful township. The hills slope in the most graceful manner; the valleys are easy and elegant; the vegetation is rich; and the prospect of the two great ranges of mountains, the lake, and the adjoining country is highly finished."

Shelburne, "a mere collection of farms," was the locale of an anecdote Dwight recounts in his "Remarks on European Travellers in America" (Volume IV of *Travels*). These European travelers, in his opinion, maligned the country. He quoted several of them at length and with scorn. Mr. Isaac Weld, who came from Dublin in 1793 and traveled extensively, was apt to make generalizations that Dwight found particularly exasperating, such as that money was the American farmer's idol "and to procure it he foregoes every self-gratification." This was based upon the poor meal Weld was given at a Shelburne farm where he stopped for dinner while traveling down Lake Champlain. "A man of common sobriety and good nature would naturally have attributed the wretchedness to their poverty," Dwight opined, "or to the recency of their settlement in the wilderness." In refutation, he quoted another traveler, "the fair-minded and gentlemanly" John Lambert, who also sought breakfast from a Shelburne farmer, was given a hearty meal, and was surprised by the variety of foods his party was offered. Weld avowed he would leave America "without entertaining the slightest wish to revisit it." And the doughty New Englander remarked: "I presume every American who reads this concluding sentence will cordially say, Amen."

One of 35 museum buildings at Shelburne, Vermont

Lake Champlain at Burlington, Vermont

Lake Champlain looking east, Camels Hump in the distance

"Splendor of landscape," to use Dwight's phraseology, "is the peculiar boast" of Lake Champlain and its valleys. At Burlington, a busy port of entry, the lake, "sixteen miles wide, extends fifty miles northward and forty southward before it reaches Crown Point, and throughout a great part of this magnificent expansion is visible. . . . In the interior, among other interesting objects, the range of the Green Mountains with its train of lofty summits commences in the south with the utmost stretch of the eye, and limiting on the east one third of the horizon, declines far northward until it becomes apparently blended with the common surface. On the west, beyond the immense field of glass formed by the waters of the lake, extends the opposite shore from its first appearance at the south until it vanishes from the eye in the northwest at the distance of forty miles. Twelve or fifteen miles from this shore ascends the first range of western mountains; about fifteen or twenty miles further, the second range; and at the same distance, the third."

Champlain Valley landscape, south of St. Albans, Vermont

Street scene in St. Albans, Vermont

Dwight and his companions left their horses at Burlington and "taking a pleasure wagon, rode to St. Albans. . . . The climate on this lake is sensibly milder than in the same latitudes on Connecticut River," Dwight noted. "The spring commences earlier, the winter later."

The travelers started out again on Monday, proceeding along the cheerful Onion River through the townships of Essex, Jericho, Bolton, and Waterbury to Middlesex. "It is impossible," Dwight commented, "for a person traveling through this cleft of the Green Mountains not to experience the most interesting emotions. The unceasing gaiety of the river and the brilliancy of its fine borders create uncommon elasticity of mind, animated thoughts, and sprightly excursions of fancy."

"Montpelier is situated at the confluence of two headwaters of Onion River," wrote Dwight. "The intervals on this stream commence at its mouth and extend with few interruptions to this place. The valley is here large enough to contain a village of perhaps thirty or forty houses within a reasonable vicinity. The hills, which are high and sudden, approach so near to the river as to form a defile rather than an open valley. About thirty or forty buildings, houses, stores, and shops, are already erected here. A few other buildings, and among them a statehouse, are begun."

Winooski (Onion) River, Vermont

Vermont hills beyond Montpelier, and the State House Dome

The State House at Montpelier, built in 1859

University of Vermont campus, Montpelier

Dwight disapproved of the choice of Montpelier for the legislature. "By that association of ideas which is so prominent a characteristic of the human mind, a little town, when the seat of government, will always impart its littleness to the legislature and to all its coadjutors. Everything must here exist on a limited scale. . . . All busy men must have their hours of relaxation; and, where refined and superior amusements cannot be obtained, will to a great extent spend those hours in such as are trifling and contemptible. The character of a town in which a legislature holds its sessions will be imparted to its members; and ultimately, to its measures. . . . [Montpelier's] situation is such as to forbid the hope of any future, material enlargement," he concluded.

Interior of meeting-house at East Montpelier Center

East Montpelier Center

In 1806 on the way to Randolph from Middlesex, Dwight traveled through Montpelier, Berlin, Williamstown, and Brookfield. "Soon after we entered this township, we came upon one of the headwaters of the White River; and, descending very rapidly, came soon to the foot of the mountains. Here we entered a narrow, flat valley, presenting a succession of verdant intervals bordering a clear, prattling stream. The hills by which it was limited were, however, neither fertile nor pleasant."

The floating bridge to Brookfield, Vermon

Back road, Brookfield

"The farmers in all these townships," Dwight noted, "live principally on the hills, the summits of which are fertile. Merchants and mechanics plant themselves in the valleys, and usually acquire ease and competence."

Spires of South Royalton, Vermont

Old Constitution House, 1777, Windsor, Vermont

On his third trip to western Vermont, in May of 1810, Dwight ascended the Connecticut River as far as Windsor, Vermont, from which he took a new turnpike cross-country to Middlebury. It gave him the "opportunity of observing the progress of blossoming on the apple tree [information that he shared with his correspondent in detail] through a circuit of 450 miles." He found the road between Windsor and Middlebury generally good. "After passing over the hills between Windsor and Woodstock, it ascends for several miles one of the branches of the Ottauquechee."

Quechee Gorge, Vermont

Woodstock, Vermont, barn

Rooftops in winter, Woodstock

Ottauquechee River at Woodstock

"The town of Woodstock is built at the junction of two branches of the Ottauquechee, at the distance of fourteen miles from Windsor. . . . It is a neat, cheerful settlement, containing a number of handsome houses, and ornamented with intervals on both streams. Woodstock is settled throughout, principally in plantations, and contained in 1790, 1,605 inhabitants . . . in 1810, 2,672."

Woodstock winter night scene

Ottauquechee River Valley

The Ottauquechee River Valley shares in the beauties of the Connecticut so eloquently and frequently described by Dwight. The falls of this river were made passable through the construction of locks and dams about 1809.

Vermont hills in winter between Woodstock and Barnard

This whole region "composed of high elevations, separated by sudden, deep, and narrow valleys, watered regularly by clean and very sprightly streams," presents a beauty that finally quieted the roving, restless spirit of settlers who found it difficult to live in quiet, well-ordered villages east of the Connecticut. In fact, they were responsible for the development of Vermont.

"In both these journeys and particularly the latter," Dwight wrote, speaking of the trips he made through Vermont in 1806 and 1810, "I found Middlebury changed into a beautiful town, consisting of about 150 houses. The inhabitants have finished a large and handsome church. The private buildings are generally neat, and in several instances handsome. The town contains a bookstore, a printing office, twelve or fifteen stores belonging to merchants and druggists, and a great number of mechanics' shops. A quarry of marble has been discovered in the bank of the river just below the bridge, a continuation of the ledge which forms the fall. It is both white and dove colored, elegantly variegated, and of a finer texture than any other which has been wrought in the United States." The academy began to "prosper from the time when it was opened, and was in the year 1800 raised by an act of incorporation into a college.... All its funds have been derived from private donations, and chiefly, if not wholly, from the inhabitants of this town. The number of students is now 110, probably as virtuous a collection of youths as can be found in any seminary in the world."

Middlebury College, summer campus on Middlebury Gap Road, Vermont

A Middlebury, Vermont, home

"Religion," wrote Dwight happily, "has prevailed in this town more than in any other in the state, and controls very obviously the manners and the character of the inhabitants in a degree uncommon and delightful. Its influence is very happily seen in the college, where the best order prevails under a discipline, exact indeed, but mild and parental. Upon the whole, Middlebury is one of the most prosperous and most virtuous towns in New England."

Their 1806 travels ended with a quick journey from Royalton, Sharon, and Hartford, Vermont, where they crossed the White River, down the Connecticut to New Haven.

MAINE

Nubble Light at York, Maine

Spring Street, Kennebunkport, Maine, looking toward North Main Street

Arundel landscape. (Arundel is the old name for the Kennebunk area.)

Mouth of the Kennebec River, Maine

Along the Kennebec River at Phippsburg, Maine

Overleaf: *Moosehead Lake, Maine*

City of Hartford, Connecticut, from the State House steps

Journey to Maine

FOR the third time, in 1807, Maine was Dwight's goal. He had gone as far as Berwick in 1796, and deeper into the state in 1797. Now he traveled there and back along nearly the same route he had taken on the first journey.

It is on this trip that, writing of Topsham's destruction, patient rebuilding by the settlers, and re-destruction by the Indians, Dwight remarks: "It seems wonderful that an individual could exist so unhappily elsewhere as to be willing to fix himself in a situation so precarious. . . .

"Until the close of the Revolutionary War Maine was considered as little less than an immense waste unfit for the habitation of man. . . . Almost all the inhabitants were merchants, land jobbers, sawyers, lumbermen, or fishermen. Both the corn and meat on which they fed were imported from Connecticut and some other states. These facts completely riveted the opinion throughout New England that the lands in Maine were of little or no value, and that farmers could not here obtain even a subsistence.

"A number of people, however, were real colonists and came to this country with the intention to cultivate the soil." They were delayed by endless title disputes and by the Indian and French wars, but finally, when they really began to farm and to build, they forged ahead. "No country in the United States," Dwight observes, "possesses in proportion to its wealth and population so great a quantity of shipping or so great a number of seamen. . . . In enterprise and activity, they will be outdone by no people on the globe."

Though at the time he was writing Maine was not yet seriously affected by events surrounding the War of 1812, she was later to suffer severely. Henry Edward Napier, lieutenant aboard the British ship *Nymphe*, described the capture of a Maine ship in his journal:

"Captured the American sloop *Three Sisters* from Frenchman's Bay . . . with shingles and plaster of Paris on board. . . . It was . . . thought expedient to take the prisoners off and burn her, which was accordingly done, although much against the inclination of . . . all on board, as the bulk of the property belonged to three poor unfortunate women. . . . They told us that their employment the last twelve months had been keeping a school at Mount Desert, the people of which place being almost unacquainted with money, had been in the habit of paying for their children's schooling in shingles (wood split into the form of tiles with which houses in America are roofed), which thus collected, they had embarked on board the *Three Sisters* intending to sell them at New London, where they hoped to receive $75.00 for their year's labour. . . . The master of the *Three Sisters* gives a deplorable account of the wretched state of trade throughout the States since the war." *

The event is revealing of Maine's poverty. The period of clipper ships and Maine's prosperous sea trade would come later. When Dwight and two alumni of Yale College set out, on September 15 of the year 1807, the great days of Maine's shipping boom lay far ahead.

*Walter Muir Whitehill, ed., *New England Blockaded in 1814: The Journal of Henry Edward Napier, Lieutenant in H.M.S. Nymphe.* (Salem: Peabody Museum, 1939).

Common at West Brookfield, Massachusetts

On the 17th of September, Dwight and his companions "entered the great western road of Massachusetts at Brookfield, and that night reached Worcester: twenty-eight miles." Taking the same road that Dwight had taken on his first journey in 1796, they proceeded to Concord, and the next day, to Andover, where they stayed until the Tuesday following.

"At Exeter," Dwight wrote, "we ate fine grapes.... This is the most northern situation in which I have known foreign grapes cultivated with success...."

At a small distance above the town, the Squamscott and Little rivers join, and these waters provided power for "eight gristmills, six sawmills, two oil mills, two chocolate mills, two fulling mills, one paper mill, one snuff mill, one slitting mill, and a furnace," plus various manufactories in 1796, but, Dwight reported, the trade was then much smaller than it had been formerly, only five or six vessels then being employed by the inhabitants in foreign commerce; and in 1810 the population had increased by only eighteen persons over that of 1775. "From Portsmouth we crossed the Piscataqua to Kittery, one of the most ancient townships in the District of Maine, bounded by this river on the southwest and the ocean on the east, and incorporated in 1653."

Front Street, the main street of Exeter, New Hampshire

Kittery Harbor, Maine

"The soil is indifferently good and the surface not unpleasant," Dwight wrote of Kittery. "It is wholly distributed into plantations, and contains three parishes, three congregations, and a Society of Friends. . . .

"York borders upon Kittery and on the ocean, and is one of the most ancient settlements in New England, having been begun in 1630. . . . The face of this township and the manner of settlement wear a general resemblance of Kittery. The northern part of it, however, is so covered with rocks and stones as to be of little use for anything besides the production of wood. It is no small misfortune to the inhabitants that thousands of acres which are now bare and yield a stinted subsistence to their cattle were not left in their forested state. The southern division has a better aspect, yet even this appears naked and bleak. . . . In the mind of an American, frequent forests, and frequent as well as fine groves, are almost necessarily associated with all his ideas of fertility, warmth, agricultural prosperity, and beauty of landscape. . . . York wears a strong appearance of stillness and solitude. The houses with few exceptions . . . have in a peculiar degree an air of antiquity."

Wilcox House, York Village, Maine

Wilcox House interior

Winter scene on York River

South Street, Kennebunkport, Maine

Twin Lights, Cape Elizabeth, Maine

Passing through Wells and Kennebunk, and stopping briefly at Saco, the travelers continued up the coast of Maine to Portland. Instead of going through Falmouth, as Dwight had done on his second trip to Maine in 1797, they traveled a new road in a direct line from Scarboro, crossing the Stroudwater near its mouth. "No place in our route, hitherto, could for its improvements be compared with Portland. . . ." Dwight declared. "Few towns in New England are equally beautiful and brilliant. Its wealth and business are probably quadrupled." It already monopolized commerce from northern New Hampshire and Vermont, as well as in Maine.

The Tate House at Stroudwater, Maine

Sweat Mansion interior, Portland. (Note the interior shutters, wood cornice, and restrained fireplace in this sitting room.)

The Brunswick, Maine, green

"Brunswick lies northeastward from Freeport, and southwestward of the Androscoggin and of Merrymeeting Bay, formed by the junction of that river with the Kennebec," Dwight wrote. "Toward the southern extremity of this township stands Bowdoin College, an institution incorporated in 1794. . . . Its buildings are two colleges, a chapel, and a presidential house. . . . Both colleges are good structures of brick. The chapel is small, but sufficiently large for the present state of the institution. It has two stories, the first of which contains the chapel, properly so-called; the second, the library, the philosophical apparatus, and a museum. The library consists of about fifteen hundred well-chosen volumes, well arranged."

Topsham, Maine, village scene

"Topsham is one of the most ancient settlements of this district, three planters having fixed themselves here about the beginning of the eighteenth century. All of them were, however, destroyed or carried into captivity together with their families. About thirty years afterward the settlement recommenced; but, being embarrassed with many difficulties and dangers, advanced very little. Until the year 1760, the savages were almost perpetually making inroads upon every defenseless settlement in this country," Dwight reported.

"The surface of this township strongly resembles that of Brunswick, from which it is separated only by the river Androscoggin."

Kennebec River at Bath, Maine

Washington Street, Bath

Day's Ferry, Maine

"The Kennebec is navigable up to Bath for ships of war carrying forty or fifty guns. But the access for such large vessels is said to be dangerous, unless they are conducted by a skillful pilot," Dwight observed. "Bath Ferry is a mile and a half above the town, where the river is three quarters of a mile in breadth. We crossed it safely in a boat of a moderate size, but not without anxiety."

In 1762 Samuel Harnden was licensed to run a ferry across the Kennebec from the north end of Bath. His son took over in 1769, and in 1784 it became known as Day's Ferry, and was still run by members of the Harnden family, who kept it up until 1830.

Kennebec River landscape at Dresden, Maine

"The country from the ferry to Dresden along the eastern bank of the Kennebec is universally undulating, the hills of no great height or extent, and without any remarkable beauty or fertility," Dwight noted unsparingly; "the surface, extremely encumbered with rocks and stones, few of them however large; the soil, loam abounding in gravel; the forest, composed chiefly of oaks and pine; the settlements, few, scattered, and unpromising; and the road difficult and discouraging, chiefly because it has been very little wrought."

A Dresden farmhouse

The Pownalborough Courthouse, now a museum, Dresden

"The river itself is beautiful," Dwight continued, in his description of the trip along the Kennebec to Dresden and Pittston, "and is from half a mile to two miles in breadth in different places. Its shores, except that they are frequently indented by the winding course of the stream, present little variety, being almost everywhere sudden acclivities, and generally covered with forest. The islands are also forested, but are cheerful objects."

The Pownalborough Courthouse, built in 1760, had already ceased holding sessions in 1794, the year of Dresden's incorporation as a town, and two years prior to Dwight's first trip to Maine. He does not mention it in his travels, though he quite likely had heard of it, since John Adams had served there as a young lawyer. It did not have the appeal of antiquity for Dwight that it does for today's traveler.

"Dresden lies along the river," he wrote. "The surface to a considerable extent is smooth, and the soil tolerably good. A moderately well-built village stands on the road, over against which we saw two or three small intervals, the more agreeably as being here very unusual."

Interiors of the courthouse

Augusta, Maine, street scene

"Augusta was the termination of our journey in this quarter," Dwight stated. "This is the shire town of Kennebec County. It was formerly a part of Hallowell, and was incorporated in the year 1797. It contains a neat Presbyterian church, an academy, a courthouse, and a jail, together with a considerable collection of good dwelling houses. These are built partly on a beautiful plain, in this country no very common object in the landscape, and partly on a declivity descending from this plain to the river. The declivity, like most of those along the Kennebec, is rather steep. The plain is a neat and smooth ground, and is elevated 150 or 200 feet above the surface of the river. The prospect around this town, and indeed its whole aspect, is handsome and very cheerful. Like Hallowell, the township lies on both sides of the river, the two parts being connected by a wooden bridge, well built on a succession of arches. Such a work in a country so recently settled is a very respectable proof of the enterprise and public spirit of the inhabitants. Augusta is at the head of ship navigation on the Kennebec. Brigs of 150 tons are loaded here."

The Capitol building at Augusta

Old house, Hallowell, Maine

Hallowell restoration. (The slatted wooden triangles protect new plants.)

"Hallowell is a very pretty town, built on an irregular or rather steep descent. This slope, though interrupted, is handsome, and furnishes more good building spots than if it had been an uniform declivity and at the same time equally steep." Dwight and his companions spent an evening and the succeeding morning with the Vaughan family, whose house still stands in Hallowell.

"Between Topsham and Brunswick, immediately above the bridge," Dwight noted, as they proceeded back toward Portland, "a ridge of rocks crosses the river Androscoggin and forms a magnificent cataract. At this place a great number of sawmills are erected. An immense quantity of logs is brought down this river and sawed at these mills. Hence they are floated two miles lower down to the head of navigation."

The Androscoggin River, looking from Topsham across to Brunswick

The mouth of the Saco River at Camp Ellis, Maine

About five miles inland, "a ridge of rocks crosses the Saco, and presents to the eye of the traveler a noble cataract, descending forty feet in a great variety of wild and magnificent torrents. On this fall is a collection of sawmills said to have cut four million feet of boards annually before the late American war, and to furnish still a very great quantity. The Saco is navigable for vessels of one hundred tons to the foot of this fall. Logs are floated down to these mills from the distance of sixty miles. As the lands on both sides are not likely soon to be cultivated, they may, if prudently managed, continue for a long time to yield a large supply of timber. The river is well furnished with fish, particularly with salmon and shad."

Biddeford Pool, Maine

The Clock Farm at Biddeford

Goat Island, from Cape Porpoise, Maine

Dwight found the Arundel road disagreeable, the houses "dismal cottages placed on little tracts of cleared ground which can never repay the labor either of the scythe or the sickle." But, he wrote, "the other parts of this township must be more advantageously situated," for the rise in population between 1790 and 1810 was unusual.

Between his first visit in 1796 and his 1807 journey, Dwight reported, "Two great fires had consumed a considerable part of Portsmouth. The vacancies produced by these conflagrations have been entirely, or nearly, filled up with several rows of handsome brick buildings, generally of four stories. Most of these are stores and, except in Boston, are as a whole not excelled in New England. Many new and beautiful houses have also been erected, and the whole aspect of the town has been essentially improved. The ecclesiastical concerns, both of Portsmouth and its neighborhood, have been less prosperous."

Middle Street, Portsmouth, New Hampshire

A Portsmouth doorway

Dwight and his friends had begun their return trip from Hallowell on September 29. During the next three days, they came down through Portland, Kennebunk, Berwick, Somersworth, and Dover, and approached Portsmouth by the Piscataqua Bridge, which Dwight admired so tremendously. They arrived during a violent storm from the northeast which had begun at half past four in the afternoon. "The rain began to descend furiously and continued through the principal part of the two succeeding days," Dwight reported. He took occasion afterward to trace the storm's progress and found it had begun at Boston at nine o'clock in the morning.

The Jackson House, Portsmouth

The Concord River at Concord, Massachusetts

From Portsmouth the travelers came down through Andover, Concord, Brimfield, and Hartford to New Haven. Dwight continued to find progress and improvement in some of the towns they went through. At Brimfield and neighboring towns particularly, he commented upon the successful use of springs and brooks for irrigation. "This, the cheapest and for meadows the best of all manures," he wrote, "might with similar advantage be spread over a great part of New England. . . . In a country where almost every farmer can not only observe and imitate, but reason also, and readily form general truths from particular facts, one would expect that such a practice would be rapidly extended. But improvement, like the heathen goddess of justice, seems everywhere to be lame at least in one foot, and to make a slow and languid progress from place to place."

NEW HAMPSHIRE
AND
RHODE ISLAND

The shore at Cliff Walk, Newport, Rhode Island

A street scene in Wickford, Rhode Island

Right: *General George De Wolfe House at Linden Place, Bristol, Rhode Island, built in 1810 by Russell Warren*

Below: *Old Slater Museum, dating from 1793, on the Blackstone River at Pawtucket, Rhode Island*

Daggett House interior, Pawtucket

Opposite: *The Merrimack River at Litchfield, New Hampshire*

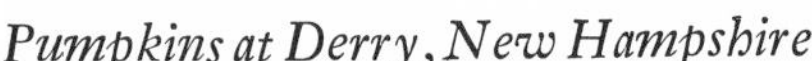

Pumpkins at Derry, New Hampshire

The Merrimack River near Concord, New Hampshire

Lake Winnipesaukee

Lake Winnipesaukee, from a hilltop in Guildford, New Hampshire

Journeys to Lake Winnipesaukee

THE last two significant New England journeys made and recorded by Timothy Dwight in 1812 and 1813 were those to Lake Winnipesaukee, the largest lake wholly contained within New England. On the first of these trips, he traveled by way of the Connecticut River, then across Massachusetts to pick up the Merrimack River, and on up along that toward the lake. On the second, he went by way of Rhode Island to Boston, Newburyport, and Portsmouth, then northwest. And in both cases he returned along the Connecticut, having gone practically to its source, at Sheffield, on the second journey.

As always, he was concerned with basic life problems that the early settlers had to deal with, and the soil was perhaps the most crucial. Of that in New Hampshire he writes: "The soil is inferior to that of the other New England states, Rhode Island excepted. In many places it is rich; and, under a superior husbandry, would easily become rich in many others. Much of it is better fitted for grazing than for agriculture. The light and warm lands might easily be rendered productive by the use of gypsum. Those which border the Merrimack are extensively of this nature. The improvement of . . . navigation will easily and cheaply furnish the inhabitants on its borders as far up as Concord or Boscawen with this valuable manure; while, on the Connecticut, it may be conveyed to Bath. When the reluctance to alter their modes of husbandry so often and so unhappily prevalent in farmers shall have been overcome, and the efficacy of gypsum shall be realized, such lands will possess a new value, and their produce be increased beyond what the proprietors could now be induced to believe."

Trade, agriculture, and government all came under Dwight's scrutiny. Trade had already become fairly extensive in New Hampshire, carried on principally with Boston, and to some extent with Hartford, Newburyport, and Portland, and was increasing. But Dwight still found the people of this state indifferent to public worship and lacking in concerted government, despite a liberal constitution and bill of rights, which, he points out, was longer than most and had many articles dealing specifically with religion.

The constitution in his opinion had its defects, "but," he writes, "they are perhaps as few as can be found in most instruments of this nature." And he concludes in his last letter upon these journeys: "A large part of the people of New Hampshire are, or lately were, immigrants from other states. Time, however, will remove the evils flowing from this source. If the public functionaries and other men of influence could be induced to unite in promoting with zeal and expansive views the public and private education of their countrymen, a superior agriculture, and such arts and manufactures as are suited to the circumstances of the country; could they harmonize in a wise and public-spirited system of government in defiance of party; could they with a single voice befriend the progress of religion, New Hampshire would ere long realize a higher reputation and more ample prosperity than the most sanguine of its citizens have hitherto expected."

Timothy Dwight started out alone on his first journey to Lake Winnipesaukee, on Tuesday, September 15, 1812.

The Parson Barnard House at North Andover, Massachusetts, in the snow

The occasion for the start of Dwight's first journey to Lake Winnipesaukee was a meeting with the American Board of Commissioners for Foreign Missions at Hartford; and the following week, at Andover, he "attended an examination of the theological students, highly honorable both to themselves and the professors." A week later, on September 29, Dwight and two Yale students, who joined him at Andover, headed for the central parts of New Hampshire.

They no doubt lingered a bit in the beautiful Massachusetts town of North Andover, then went on through Bradford and Haverhill, crossed into New Hampshire and continued to Atkinson and Hampstead and on to Chester. "The surface of the country from Haverhill to Chester is a succession of handsome hills and valleys, everywhere arched," Dwight began, using one of his favorite descriptive phrases. "The soil is a light brown loam, moderately good, and universally cultivated, except where handsome groves, interspersed at very agreeable distances, form one fine feature in the landscape. Another still finer is made up of distant mountains, sometimes very noble, seen successively from the summits of the hills. . . . The houses and barns throughout this region are generally good, and . . . sufficiently indicate that the inhabitants are in comfortable circumstances."

"On Wednesday we proceeded to Concord," Dwight wrote. "The road for fifteen miles to Pembroke is a turnpike, lately formed through a tract almost absolutely uninhabited, and alternately covered with forests of maple, pine, and oak. . . . All of them are dull and dismal, and the whole region is one of the most uninviting which I have met with. . . . Pembroke is built principally on a hill, declining easily toward the southwest. . . . The prospect from the hill is fine." The road, which was generally firm and good, lay almost wholly on a pine plain.

Pembroke, New Hampshire, street scene

"Concord is pleasantly situated on both sides of the Merrimack," Dwight continued. "The town is built principally on the western side upon a single street, near two miles in length, and running parallel with the river. Its site is a handsome plain, limited westward by hills at the distance of perhaps half a mile, and eastward by an interval which is both pleasant and fertile. The prospect from this town up and down the river is extensive and interesting, and the scenery around it is cheerful. The intervals within the limits of the township amount to about one thousand acres, the current price of which, by the acre, is from sixty to one hundred and twenty dollars."

Concord, New Hampshire, on the Merrimack

State Capitol at Concord

"Since the Revolution, Concord, much more frequently than any other town in New Hampshire, has been the place where the Legislature has held its sessions, and will probably be the permanent seat of government," Dwight rightly predicted.

A quiet street on the grounds of St. Paul's School at Concord

"The western part of the township, separated from the town by a pine ridge, is excellent land," Dwight reported. (And it still has its quiet, wide lawns.) "The public buildings are the church, courthouse, a well-built schoolhouse, and the state prison… a noble edifice of beautiful granite, which abounds in the vicinity. It is a copy of the state prison at Charlestown, both in the materials and the structure."

Traveling along the Merrimack through Boscawen, and skirting Salisbury, Dwight and his companions crossed two rivers and entered Sanbornton, the site of an Indian fortification "which is remarkable for being formed of five enclosures," he commented. The road was in various places stony and disagreeable. "It ought however to be observed to the honor of the inhabitants of this state that, although the population is sparse, they are making their roads universally very good. In the parts where they were originally the worst, they have already made them to a great extent excellent, in the manner of turnpikes.... These parts they are proceeding as fast as may be to unite, by filling up the interstices according to the same plan. When the design is completed, New Hampshire . . . will have the merit, which I believe is singular, of accomplishing so difficult an object by statute labor."

Sanbornton town buildings, New Hampshire

Indian statue, Endicott Rock, Weirs Beach, New Hampshire, marker of the headwaters of the Merrimack River

Excursion boat "Mount Washington" on Lake Winnipesaukee, New Hampshire

Early morning, Lake Winnipesaukee

Lake Winnipesaukee, the highlight of each of Dwight's last two recorded voyages to New Hampshire, they saw in full view for the first time from a house at Center Harbor. "I have elsewhere mentioned the want of curiosity of the New England people concerning things which are their own, particularly concerning the fine objects of their own country. The fact that New England abounds with elegant pieces of water has not even made its appearance in books either of geographers or travelers. At least I know not where it has appeared. Yet there is probably no country which is more frequently or more highly adorned with this exquisite beauty of landscape. Of this lake, which has been generally supposed to be the largest of all those whose waters are wholly included within the limits of New England, I have never heard, nor seen, a syllable, except a few slight geographical notices concerning its length, breadth, position. . . . Indeed a few observations made to me concerning this subject by my father when I was a child were not improbably more than all that I have heard concerning it from that time to the present."

Boats at Lake Winnipesaukee

From a hill on the road toward Plymouth, their next goal, Winnipesaukee was even more beautiful, Dwight noted. "Not a breath disturbed the leaves or ruffled the surface of the waters.... Mildness tempered the heat, and serenity hushed the world into universal quiet. The Winnipesaukee was an immense field of glass, silvered by the luster which floated on its surface." They crossed the Pemigewasset River in a boat and reached Plymouth at sunset. Dwight was fascinated by the number of ponds in the area, as he was by the islands in Lake Winnipesaukee. "Like those in Lake George and in Casco Bay," he remarked drily, "they are here declared to be three hundred and sixty-five. Without supposing the number of days in the year to have been consulted on this subject . . . we may rationally conclude that the number in each of the cases is considerable."

Pemigewasset River just south of Plymouth, New Hampshire

There was probably no *West* Rumney in Dwight's time, for in Rumney proper, through which they rode the next day, the census of 1810 had recorded only 765 inhabitants. After they left Plymouth, their route had ascended Baker River, "a large and beautiful millstream," one of the tributaries of the Pemigewasset. "The scenery in this part of our journey was formed by the valley, frequently ornamented by intervals at the bottom, and a succession of hills by which it was bordered, rising at times to a mountainous height."

View of West Rumney, New Hampshire

They began gradually to ascend the Lyme Range after their route broke away from Baker River; and the villages became much less populous. Dwight provided the 1790, 1800, and 1810 census figures, as he did for most of the towns he passed through. Their variations would make an interesting graph of the settlement of New England. For example, in Wentworth the 1810 figure was only 645; in the rich farmland towns of Sanbornton and Gilmanton, the figures jumped from 1,587 and 2,613 in 1790, to 2,884 and 4,388 in 1810, respectively.

Baker River at Wentworth, New Hampshire

Wentworth green

Haverhill, New Hampshire

White Mountains—view north of Haverhill

"Finer scenery can scarcely be imagined than that which is spread throughout this region," Dwight wrote, as the travelers descended into the Connecticut River Valley of western New Hampshire. "Haverhill has become a beautiful village." On his journey to the Canada line in 1803, Dwight had devoted an entire letter to the valley itself, which he described as a series of openings, or expansions, along the whole river. Besides the four great expansions into which he divided it, "there are beautiful openings at Walpole, Charlestown, Windsor, Orford, Haverhill, Stratford, and Colebrook," he wrote. "Several of these, particularly those at Charlestown, Haverhill, and Colebrook, are from ten to twenty miles in length."

Dwight and his companions crossed the Connecticut on a toll bridge, and at Newbury, "having obtained a convenient wagon and a discreet young man to drive it, made an excursion into the interior of Vermont through the townships of Ryegate, Barnet, St. Johnsbury, and Lyndon into Sheffield. The first day, we rode twenty-three miles after dinner. The second, we labored hard to finish twenty-four. The third, we returned to Wells River: forty-two miles. The first twelve or fifteen, our journey lay along Connecticut River, and then as much more along the Posoomsuck [Passumpsic]; the remainder was continual ascent and descent of lofty hills."

Connecticut River at Bradford, Vermont

"In St. Johnsbury," Dwight noted, "is a plain about half a mile in diameter, remarkable for being the only spot of this nature throughout the whole distance.... The weather, although it was only so late as the 5th and 6th of October, we found intensely cold. It snowed and rained alternately on both days, and on the morning of Wednesday the ground was hard frozen. The maize had been chiefly destroyed by a succession of frosts during the preceding month; and, what I had never heard of at this season of the year before, the wheat had in several instances been killed by frost about the 20th of August.

"The summer was the coldest which I ever knew. In grounds which were not warm and particularly favorable, the maize scarcely attained half its proper growth; and of that which grew well, not more than two thirds or three fourths arrived at maturity.... Most of the summer and autumnal fruits were also shriveled and insipid."

Bandstand on the green at St. Johnsbury, Vermont

The Passumpsic River at St. Johnsbury

"On the Passumpsic, as well as on the Connecticut," wrote Dwight, "are many rich and handsome intervals." In a study of the latter river, to which Dwight had devoted an earlier letter, he described it as being about 410 miles long, with 16 principal tributaries, among which he listed the Passumpsic, one of those on the west, as about 40 miles long.

The Orford, New Hampshire, Social Library

They started back from Wells River, where they had "found a good hospitable inn," and drove through Newbury and Orford to Hanover the first day; and the next day reached Windsor. On the way, "the horse belonging to my companions was frightened by a wagon," Dwight reported, "and running off a causey, overturned their chaise." They were unharmed, but the incident reveals that apparently they no longer rode horseback on these journeys, except for special excursions off the beaten path. No doubt this was partly because of Dwight's increasing age, but also because the roads were so much better than when he began his travels.

Paradise Pond, Smith College, Northampton, Massachusetts

Warehouse Point, Windsor, Connecticut

Since Dwight had an appointment to serve as Connecticut delegate to a convention of clergymen at Windsor a week later, his companions went on. No doubt he occupied the week in profitable investigations. Three days after the meeting, he reached Northampton, Massachusetts, where he spent the weekend, before starting out on the last lap of his journey. It must have presented an enjoyable atmosphere to Dwight. "The people of Northampton have always been particularly friendly to learning," he had declared previously; and several of its most notable citizens were his ancestors.

Corners and spires at Providence, Rhode Island

The Rhode Island State House, Providence

Almost a year later, on September 6, 1813, in the company of two Yale students, Timothy Dwight entered upon his second journey to Winnipesaukee. This time, he approached the lake by way of Hartford and Providence.

One of Dwight's infrequent references to the War of 1812 was in his Preface to the *Travels* when, in acknowledging the help he had received from Yale students who accompanied him, and wrote his notes for him, and enabled him to continue investigations he would otherwise have had to give up because of failing eyes, he added: "The turmoil excited between this country and Great Britain threw, however, many discouragements in my way. Without expatiating upon the subject, I shall only observe that the book would have been finished several years sooner, had it not been for this hindrance." Still, he must have recognized the stimulus that the Embargo Act and consequent shortage of European goods had upon manufacturing in New England. Providence, where Slater's cotton mills had been in existence since 1793 and many other products were being manufactured, was a bustling center of commerce in 1813.

At Charlestown, Massachusetts, two other Yale men joined Dwight's party. In an earlier trip he had written at some length about this town, "long to be remembered in history as the scene of the first regular battle in the Revolutionary War." The horror of the awful carnage was increased by the flames that destroyed the whole town, by order of the British general, Thomas Gage. After it was burned, according to Dwight, the proprietors had the chance to make it "one of the most beautiful towns in the world," but for lack of decisive direction, it was allowed to develop haphazardly. "Its present location," he stated baldly in 1797, "is almost only preposterous." However, he often visited there on his way to and from upper New England.

Fleur de Lis Building, Providence

Charlestown, Massachusetts

On his way to Salem and Newburyport, Massachusetts, Dwight visited the theological seminary in Andover, in which he always took particular interest. He found it prospering, with fifty students. But "the country between Andover and Salem, except the township of Danvers, is dull and spiritless," he declared. "Its surface is undulating, but without beauty. The soil, the enclosures, and the buildings are indifferent."

The Richard Derby House, Salem, Massachusetts

Merrimacport, Massachusetts

The country between Newburyport and Bradford, lying twelve miles along the Merrimack, was a different matter. Its "succession of hills and valleys, both almost universally and elegantly arched, the concave of the latter being little else than a counterpart to the convex of the former," revived Dwight's spirits. He was happy also to learn of the successful renewal of the culture of wheat by two farmers in this region. For more than a hundred years it had been "proverbially and universally asserted that wheat could not come to perfection throughout most of the eastern half of Massachusetts. The charm is now broken," Dwight declared, "and the authority of this gray-haired prejudice destroyed."

From Bradford, they "proceeded to Essex bridge, newly built upon strong iron chains, probably the best mode of building bridges hitherto adopted in this country when the water is deep and the channel not very wide."

Village green, Bradford, Massachusetts

Opposite: *The First Religious Society steeple, Newburyport, Massachusetts, built in 1801*

Chain bridge over the Merrimack near Newburyport

The Old Country Store, Moultonborough, New Hampshire

Lake Winnipesaukee from Red Mountain

The travelers rode on to Lake Winnipesaukee through Dover, New Hampshire (which Dwight found considerably improved and beautified over his last visit), Rochester, Middleton, Wolfeboro, Tuftonboro, and Moultonboro. "We determined on an excursion to the summit of the Red Mountain, for the purpose of taking a complete view of the Winnipesaukee, or, as I shall henceforth call it, the *Wentworth*. Accordingly we set out on horseback at an early hour, and rode quite to the highest point. The ascent was often steep and difficult, but nowhere impracticable. When we had reached the summit, we found a prospect worth not only the trouble of the ascent, but that of our whole journey.... Southwestward, at the distance of seventy miles, appeared the conical summit of Monadnock, like a blue cloud in the skirt of the horizon."

"On the west," Dwight continued his observations from Red Mountain, "also immediately beneath our feet, lay Squam Lake, which I shall take the liberty to call by the name of *Sullivan*, from Major General Sullivan, formerly president of this state. This sheet of water is inferior in beauty to no other; and is richly furnished with its suite of islands, points, and promontories, among the least of which was the mountain whence we gained our prospect. . . . Nothing could be more cheerful than the appearance of these fields of water, extending on both sides of the promontory where we stood between thirty and forty miles. The whole scene was made up of the most beautiful parts, and these were so arranged as to compose a finished whole. But the impression was immeasurably enhanced by the objects with which these waters were surrounded. The expansion was vast and noble."

Squam Lake, New Hampshire

Holderness, New Hampshire, landscape

After they had feasted themselves upon the prospect as long as their circumstances would permit, the group resumed their journey toward the Connecticut River by way of Holderness, Plymouth, and Rumney. From a high ground in Holderness they had a "spacious prospect of the surrounding region, composed of valleys, hills, and mountains." The farmer in Dwight never ceased to note the worth of the land they traveled. According to him, the soil throughout most of the area they covered that day was good grazing ground.

Street scene at Walpole, New Hampshire

The Connecticut River Valley at Northfield, Massachusetts

New Haven

The next morning they rode to Piermont for dinner at a farmhouse where they had stayed the previous year, situated in "an elegant solitude." From this point, his horse having become suddenly lame, he traveled by the shortest possible route direct to Orford and down the Connecticut, while his companions took a more circuitous road, rejoining him occasionally, on his way through Walpole and through Northfield, Northampton, and Springfield, Massachusetts, to New Haven.

So ended Timothy Dwight's last long journey down the beloved river.

INDEX OF PHOTOGRAPHS

Travels in New England, Volumes I & II,

was designed by Klaus Gemming of New Haven, Connecticut.
It is set in Linotype Janson with Centaur and Arrighi for display
by Finn Typographic Service, Inc., of Stamford, Connecticut.
The text paper is Warren's 1854 Medium Offset, purchased from
Lindenmeyr Paper Corporation, Long Island City, New York.
The book was printed and bound by Halliday Lithograph Corporation
of West Hanover, Massachusetts.

Barre Publishing